SECURITY+ EXAM PASS (SY0-701)

SECURITY ARCHITECTURE, THREAT IDENTIFICATION, RISK MANAGEMENT, OPERATIONS

4 BOOKS IN 1

BOOK 1
FOUNDATIONS OF SECURITY ARCHITECTURE: A BEGINNER'S GUIDE TO SY0-701

BOOK 2
MASTERING THREAT IDENTIFICATION: STRATEGIES AND TECHNIQUES FOR SY0-701

BOOK 3
RISK MANAGEMENT ESSENTIALS: NAVIGATING SECURITY CHALLENGES IN SY0-701

BOOK 4
ADVANCED SECURITY OPERATIONS: IMPLEMENTING SY0-701 BEST PRACTICES AND BEYOND

ROB BOTWRIGHT

Published by Rob Botwright
Library of Congress Cataloging-in-Publication Data
ISBN 978-1-83938-785-2
Cover design by Rizzo

Disclaimer

The contents of this book are based on extensive research and the best available historical sources. However, the author and publisher make no claims, promises, or guarantees about the accuracy, completeness, or adequacy of the information contained herein. The information in this book is provided on an "as is" basis, and the author and publisher disclaim any and all liability for any errors, omissions, or inaccuracies in the information or for any actions taken in reliance on such information. The opinions and views expressed in this book are those of the author and do not necessarily reflect the official policy or position of any organization or individual mentioned in this book. Any reference to specific people, places, or events is intended only to provide historical context and is not intended to defame or malign any group, individual, or entity. The information in this book is intended for educational and entertainment purposes only. It is not intended to be a substitute for professional advice or judgment. Readers are encouraged to conduct their own research and to seek professional advice where appropriate. Every effort has been made to obtain necessary permissions and acknowledgments for all images and other copyrighted material used in this book. Any errors or omissions in this regard are unintentional, and the author and publisher will correct them in future editions.

BOOK 1 - FOUNDATIONS OF SECURITY ARCHITECTURE: A BEGINNER'S GUIDE TO SY0-701

BOOK 2 - MASTERING THREAT IDENTIFICATION: STRATEGIES AND TECHNIQUES FOR SY0-701

BOOK 3 - RISK MANAGEMENT ESSENTIALS: NAVIGATING SECURITY CHALLENGES IN SY0-701

BOOK 4 - ADVANCED SECURITY OPERATIONS: IMPLEMENTING SY0-701 BEST PRACTICES AND BEYOND

Introduction

Welcome to the "Security+ Exam Pass: (SY0-701) Security Architecture, Threat Identification, Risk Management, Operations" book bundle. This comprehensive collection of books is designed to equip readers with the knowledge and skills needed to excel in the field of cybersecurity and pass the SY0-701 exam with confidence.

In an increasingly interconnected world where cyber threats continue to evolve and proliferate, cybersecurity has become a critical priority for organizations of all sizes and industries. The Security+ certification, offered by CompTIA, is widely recognized as a benchmark for validating cybersecurity expertise, making it a valuable credential for professionals seeking to advance their careers in the field.

This book bundle comprises four distinct volumes, each focusing on key aspects of cybersecurity:

"Foundations of Security Architecture: A Beginner's Guide to SY0-701" lays the groundwork for understanding the principles of security architecture, providing readers with a solid foundation in the fundamental concepts and practices of building secure systems and networks.

"Mastering Threat Identification: Strategies and Techniques for SY0-701" dives deep into the realm of threat identification, offering readers practical strategies and techniques for identifying and mitigating various types of cybersecurity threats, from malware and phishing attacks to insider threats and beyond.

"Risk Management Essentials: Navigating Security Challenges in SYO-701" explores the critical role of risk management in cybersecurity, guiding readers through the process of assessing, prioritizing, and mitigating security risks to protect their organizations from potential threats.

"Advanced Security Operations: Implementing SYO-701 Best Practices and Beyond" takes readers beyond the basics, delving into advanced security operations and best practices. From incident response planning to security automation, this volume provides readers with the tools and techniques needed to streamline security operations and respond effectively to security incidents.

Whether you're a beginner looking to establish a solid foundation in cybersecurity or an experienced professional seeking to enhance your skills and advance your career, the "Security+ Exam Pass: (SYO-701) Security Architecture, Threat Identification, Risk Management, Operations" book bundle is your comprehensive guide to mastering the essential concepts and practices of cybersecurity. Let's embark on this journey together and prepare to excel in the dynamic and ever-evolving field of cybersecurity.

BOOK 1
FOUNDATIONS OF SECURITY ARCHITECTURE
A BEGINNER'S GUIDE TO SY0-701

ROB BOTWRIGHT

Chapter 1: Introduction to Security Fundamentals

The security threat landscape is a dynamic and ever-evolving ecosystem that encompasses a wide range of potential risks and vulnerabilities. It is characterized by a constant influx of new threats and attack vectors, making it essential for organizations to stay vigilant and proactive in their security measures. One of the key aspects of understanding the security threat landscape is recognizing the diverse range of threats that exist in the digital realm. From common threats such as phishing attacks and malware infections to more sophisticated threats like advanced persistent threats (APTs) and zero-day exploits, the landscape is vast and multifaceted.

To effectively navigate this landscape, organizations must have a comprehensive understanding of the different types of cyber threats that they may encounter. This includes understanding the tactics, techniques, and procedures (TTPs) employed by threat actors to infiltrate networks and compromise data. For example, understanding the anatomy of malware is crucial for identifying and mitigating potential threats. This involves recognizing the different types of malware, such as viruses, worms, Trojans, and ransomware, and understanding how they propagate and infect systems.

In addition to malware, organizations must also be aware of the various forms of social engineering tactics that threat actors use to manipulate individuals into divulging sensitive information or performing unauthorized actions. Common social engineering techniques include phishing emails, pretexting, baiting, and tailgating. By educating employees about these tactics and implementing robust security awareness training programs, organizations can mitigate the risk of falling victim to social engineering attacks.

Another important aspect of the security threat landscape is the emergence of advanced persistent threats (APTs). APTs are sophisticated cyber attacks that are typically conducted by well-funded and highly skilled threat actors, such as nation-state actors or organized crime groups. These attacks are often characterized by their stealthy nature and long-term persistence within a targeted network. Detecting and mitigating APTs requires a combination of advanced threat detection techniques, such as behavior analysis, threat hunting, and endpoint detection and response (EDR) solutions.

Furthermore, organizations must be vigilant in monitoring and analyzing threat intelligence feeds to stay abreast of the latest threats and vulnerabilities. Threat intelligence feeds provide valuable information about emerging threats, new attack techniques, and indicators of compromise (IOCs) that can help organizations identify and respond to potential security incidents. By leveraging threat intelligence feeds and integrating them into their security operations, organizations can enhance their ability to detect, prevent, and respond to cyber threats effectively.

In addition to external threats, organizations must also be mindful of insider threats – individuals within the organization who may pose a risk to security. Insider threats can take various forms, including malicious insiders who intentionally sabotage systems or steal sensitive data, as well as unwitting insiders who inadvertently compromise security through negligent or careless behavior. Implementing robust insider threat detection and mitigation measures, such as user behavior analytics (UBA) and data loss prevention (DLP) solutions, is essential for protecting against insider threats.

Moreover, as organizations increasingly migrate their infrastructures to the cloud, they must also consider the unique security challenges posed by cloud environments. Cloud security operations require a different approach compared to traditional on-premises environments, with an emphasis on securing cloud-native applications and infrastructure, implementing strong identity and access management (IAM) controls, and ensuring compliance with regulatory requirements. Deploying cloud-native security tools and leveraging cloud-specific security services, such as AWS GuardDuty or Azure Security Center, can help organizations enhance their cloud security posture and mitigate the risks associated with cloud adoption.

Overall, gaining a comprehensive understanding of the security threat landscape is essential for organizations to develop effective cybersecurity strategies and mitigate the risks posed by cyber threats. By staying informed about the latest threat trends, leveraging advanced threat detection techniques, and implementing robust security controls, organizations can enhance their ability to protect their sensitive data and assets from cyber attacks.

The principles of confidentiality, integrity, and availability (CIA) are fundamental concepts in the field of information security, providing a framework for safeguarding sensitive data and ensuring the reliability and usability of systems and resources. Confidentiality refers to the protection of information from unauthorized access or disclosure, ensuring that only authorized individuals or entities have access to sensitive data. One of the most common techniques used to enforce confidentiality is encryption, which involves transforming plaintext data into ciphertext using cryptographic algorithms and keys, rendering it unreadable to anyone without the appropriate decryption key. For example, organizations can use the OpenSSL command-line tool to encrypt sensitive files or data streams using symmetric or asymmetric encryption algorithms such as AES or RSA. By encrypting data both at rest and in transit, organizations can prevent unauthorized individuals or malicious actors from intercepting or accessing sensitive information.

Additionally, access control mechanisms, such as access control lists (ACLs) and role-based access control (RBAC), can be implemented to restrict access to confidential data based on user roles, permissions, and privileges. For instance, organizations can use the chmod command in Unix-based operating systems to set permissions on files and directories, allowing only authorized users or groups to read, write, or execute specific files. By enforcing strict access controls and least privilege principles, organizations can minimize the risk of unauthorized access and protect the confidentiality of sensitive information.

Integrity, on the other hand, refers to the accuracy, consistency, and trustworthiness of data, ensuring that information remains unaltered and reliable throughout its lifecycle. One of the key techniques used to enforce data integrity is the use of cryptographic hash functions, which generate unique hash values or checksums for data sets, allowing users to verify the integrity of the data by comparing the computed hash value with the original hash value. For example, organizations can use the sha256sum command in Linux to compute the SHA-256 hash value of files or directories and verify their integrity. By regularly computing and comparing hash values, organizations can detect any unauthorized modifications or tampering of data and take appropriate corrective actions to restore data integrity.

Moreover, digital signatures can be used to provide cryptographic proof of data integrity and authenticity, allowing users to verify the origin and integrity of digital documents or messages. Digital signatures are generated using public-key cryptography, where the sender signs a message using their private key, and the recipient can verify the signature using the sender's public key. For instance, organizations can use the GnuPG (GNU Privacy Guard) command-line tool to generate digital signatures for files or email messages and verify their authenticity using the sender's public key. By digitally signing critical documents or communications, organizations can ensure the integrity and authenticity of their data and prevent unauthorized alterations or forgeries.

Furthermore, organizations must ensure the availability of information and resources to authorized users when needed, minimizing downtime and disruptions to business operations. Redundancy and fault tolerance mechanisms, such as data replication, mirroring, and failover clustering, can be implemented to mitigate the risk of service outages and ensure high availability of critical systems and services. For example, organizations can use the rsync command in Unix-based operating systems to synchronize files and directories between multiple servers or storage devices, ensuring data redundancy and availability. By deploying redundant infrastructure components and implementing disaster recovery plans, organizations can maintain continuous access to data and services even in the event of hardware failures, natural disasters, or cyber attacks.

In summary, the principles of confidentiality, integrity, and availability (CIA) form the cornerstone of effective information security practices, guiding organizations in their efforts to protect sensitive data, maintain data integrity, and ensure the availability of critical resources. By implementing robust encryption, access control, data integrity, and availability measures, organizations can mitigate the risk of data breaches, unauthorized access, data tampering, and service disruptions, safeguarding their assets and maintaining the trust and confidence of their stakeholders.

Chapter 2: Understanding Network Security Principles

Network defense mechanisms are essential components of any organization's cybersecurity strategy, comprising a variety of tools, techniques, and best practices designed to protect networks from cyber threats and unauthorized access. One of the fundamental network defense mechanisms is the implementation of firewalls, which act as gatekeepers between internal networks and the internet, filtering incoming and outgoing traffic based on predefined rules and policies. Firewalls can be deployed as hardware appliances or software applications and can be configured using command-line interface (CLI) commands such as iptables in Linux or netsh in Windows to define access control lists (ACLs) and filter network traffic based on IP addresses, ports, and protocols. By enforcing strict firewall rules, organizations can prevent unauthorized access to network resources and block malicious traffic, reducing the risk of cyber attacks and data breaches.

Another key network defense mechanism is intrusion detection and prevention systems (IDPS), which monitor network traffic for signs of suspicious or malicious activity and take proactive measures to block or mitigate potential threats. IDPS can be deployed in various network locations, including at the network perimeter, on internal network segments, and on individual hosts, to provide comprehensive threat detection and prevention capabilities. CLI commands such as snort or suricata can be used to configure and manage open-source IDPS solutions, allowing organizations to create custom intrusion detection rules and policies tailored to their specific security requirements. By deploying IDPS solutions, organizations can detect and respond to network intrusions in real-time, minimizing the impact of cyber attacks and enhancing overall network security posture. Moreover, network segmentation is a crucial network defense mechanism that involves dividing a large network into smaller, isolated segments or zones to contain the spread of cyber threats and limit the scope of potential security incidents. Network segmentation can be implemented using VLANs (virtual LANs) or network access control lists (ACLs) to segregate traffic and enforce access controls between different network segments. CLI commands such as vlan in Cisco IOS or ip route in Linux can be used to create VLANs and define routing policies between network segments, ensuring that only authorized users and devices have access to specific resources and services. By implementing network segmentation, organizations can minimize the risk of lateral movement by attackers within their networks and improve overall network resilience against cyber threats.

Furthermore, network monitoring and logging are essential components of effective network defense, providing visibility into network activity and enabling organizations to detect and investigate security incidents in a timely manner. Network monitoring tools such as Wireshark or tcpdump can be used to capture and analyze network traffic in real-time, allowing security analysts to identify abnormal patterns, unauthorized access attempts, or signs of malicious activity. CLI commands such as tcpdump -i eth0 -n port 80 can be used to capture and display HTTP traffic on a specific network interface, facilitating the identification of potential security threats or vulnerabilities. Additionally, logging and auditing mechanisms can be configured on network devices such as routers, switches, and firewalls to record events and activities for forensic analysis and compliance purposes. By maintaining comprehensive logs and audit trails, organizations can track network activity, investigate security incidents, and ensure compliance with regulatory requirements.

Moreover, network access control (NAC) solutions play a critical role in enforcing security policies and controlling access to network resources based on the identity, device posture, and security posture of users and devices. NAC solutions can be deployed as standalone appliances or integrated into existing network infrastructure to authenticate users and devices, enforce access controls, and remediate non-compliant endpoints. CLI commands such as nmap or arp can be used to scan the network for unauthorized devices or open ports, allowing organizations to identify potential security risks and enforce network access policies accordingly. By implementing NAC solutions, organizations can prevent unauthorized access to sensitive network resources, mitigate the risk of insider threats, and maintain compliance with security policies and regulations.

Additionally, network encryption is a critical network defense mechanism that helps protect data in transit from eavesdropping, interception, and tampering by encrypting network communications using cryptographic algorithms and protocols. Secure sockets layer (SSL) and transport layer security (TLS) protocols are commonly used to encrypt web traffic over HTTPS connections, providing confidentiality, integrity, and authentication for sensitive data transmitted over the internet. CLI commands such as openssl or keytool can be used to generate SSL/TLS certificates, configure SSL/TLS settings, and manage cryptographic keys for securing network communications. By implementing network encryption, organizations can ensure the privacy and security of sensitive data transmitted over public networks, reducing the risk of data interception and unauthorized access by malicious actors.

Furthermore, network access control lists (ACLs) are a fundamental network defense mechanism that enables organizations to control traffic flow and enforce security policies at the network perimeter, on routers, switches, and firewalls. ACLs can be configured to permit or deny traffic based on various criteria, including source and destination IP addresses, ports, protocols, and traffic direction. CLI commands such as access-list in Cisco IOS or ip access-group in Juniper Junos can be used to create, modify, and apply ACLs to network interfaces or firewall policies, allowing organizations to filter incoming and outgoing traffic and block unauthorized access attempts. By implementing ACLs, organizations can reduce the attack surface of their networks, protect critical resources from unauthorized access, and enforce security policies to mitigate the risk of cyber threats and data breaches.

In summary, network defense mechanisms are essential components of any organization's cybersecurity strategy, providing the foundation for protecting networks from cyber threats and unauthorized access. By implementing a combination of firewalls, intrusion detection and prevention systems (IDPS), network segmentation, monitoring and logging, network access control (NAC), network encryption, and network access control lists (ACLs), organizations can establish robust defenses to safeguard their networks, data, and resources against a wide range of cyber threats. Additionally, regular security assessments, vulnerability scans, and penetration testing can help organizations identify and address weaknesses in their network defenses, ensuring continuous improvement and resilience against evolving cyber threats.

Symmetric and asymmetric encryption are two fundamental cryptographic techniques used to secure data and communications in modern computer systems, each with its own strengths and weaknesses. Symmetric encryption, also known as secret-key encryption, uses a single shared key to both encrypt and decrypt data, making it faster and more efficient than asymmetric encryption for large volumes of data. The openssl command can be used to generate symmetric encryption keys, such as AES (Advanced Encryption Standard) or DES (Data Encryption Standard), and encrypt plaintext data using the generated key and an encryption algorithm. For example, the openssl enc - aes-256-cbc -in plaintext.txt -out ciphertext.enc -k my_secret_key command can be used to encrypt a file named plaintext.txt using AES-256 encryption with a shared secret key, and store the encrypted data in a file named ciphertext.enc. By using symmetric encryption, organizations can protect sensitive data and communications from unauthorized access or interception, ensuring confidentiality and privacy.

However, symmetric encryption requires the secure exchange of secret keys between communicating parties, which can be challenging to manage and distribute securely, particularly in large-scale or distributed systems. Key management techniques, such as key exchange protocols, key generation algorithms, and key rotation policies, can be used to securely generate, distribute, and revoke symmetric encryption keys. For example, the Diffie-Hellman key exchange protocol can be used to securely negotiate a shared secret key between two parties over an insecure communication channel, without the need for pre-shared keys or secure key distribution mechanisms. By implementing robust key management practices, organizations can mitigate the risk of unauthorized access to symmetric encryption keys and protect their encrypted data and communications from interception or decryption by malicious actors.

In contrast, asymmetric encryption, also known as public-key encryption, uses a pair of mathematically related keys — a public key and a private key — to encrypt and decrypt data, providing stronger security guarantees and eliminating the need for secure key exchange mechanisms. The openssl command can be used to generate asymmetric encryption key pairs, such as RSA (Rivest-Shamir-Adleman) or Elliptic Curve Cryptography (ECC), and encrypt plaintext data using the recipient's public key and an encryption algorithm. For example, the openssl rsautl -encrypt -in plaintext.txt -out ciphertext.enc -pubin -inkey recipient_public_key.pem command can be used to encrypt a file named plaintext.txt using RSA encryption with the recipient's public key stored in a file named recipient_public_key.pem, and store the encrypted data in a file named ciphertext.enc. By using asymmetric encryption, organizations can securely exchange encrypted data and communications with external parties or untrusted networks, without the need for pre-shared keys or secure key distribution mechanisms.

Furthermore, asymmetric encryption provides additional security benefits, such as digital signatures and key authentication, which can be used to verify the integrity and authenticity of encrypted data and the identity of communicating parties. Digital signatures are generated using the sender's private key and can be verified using the sender's public key, providing cryptographic proof of data integrity and authenticity. The openssl command can be used to generate digital signatures for files or messages using the sender's private key and verify the signatures using the sender's public key. For example, the openssl dgst -sha256 -sign sender_private_key.pem   -out   signature.sha256 plaintext.txt command can be used to generate a digital signature for a file named plaintext.txt using the sender's private key stored in a file named sender_private_key.pem, and store the signature in a file named signature.sha256. By using digital signatures, organizations can ensure the integrity and authenticity of encrypted data and communications, protecting against data tampering or forgery by malicious actors.

Moreover, asymmetric encryption enables secure key exchange mechanisms, such as key encapsulation, key agreement, and key transport protocols, which can be used to securely negotiate symmetric encryption keys between communicating parties without the need for pre-shared keys or secure key distribution mechanisms. For example, the Diffie-Hellman key exchange protocol can be used to securely negotiate a shared symmetric encryption key between two parties over an insecure communication channel, using their respective public and private keys. By leveraging asymmetric encryption for key exchange, organizations can establish secure and confidential communications channels with external parties or untrusted networks, ensuring the confidentiality, integrity, and authenticity of encrypted data and communications.

In summary, symmetric and asymmetric encryption are two fundamental cryptographic techniques used to secure data and communications in modern computer systems, each with its own strengths and weaknesses.

Symmetric encryption is faster and more efficient for encrypting large volumes of data but requires secure key exchange mechanisms to distribute shared secret keys securely. Asymmetric encryption provides stronger security guarantees and eliminates the need for secure key exchange mechanisms but is slower and less efficient than symmetric encryption for large volumes of data. By understanding the strengths and weaknesses of symmetric and asymmetric encryption, organizations can choose the appropriate cryptographic techniques and key management practices to protect their sensitive data and communications from unauthorized access or interception by malicious actors.

Chapter 3: Basics of Cryptography and Encryption

Symmetric and asymmetric encryption are two fundamental cryptographic techniques used to secure data and communications in modern computer systems, each with its own strengths and weaknesses. Symmetric encryption, also known as secret-key encryption, utilizes a single shared key for both encryption and decryption processes, making it efficient for large volumes of data. To encrypt data symmetrically, one can use commands such as OpenSSL, which allows the generation of encryption keys and encryption of plaintext data using these keys and specific algorithms. For instance, the command "openssl enc -aes-256-cbc -in plaintext.txt -out ciphertext.enc -k my_secret_key" encrypts a file named plaintext.txt using AES-256 encryption with a shared secret key and stores the encrypted data in a file named ciphertext.enc. Symmetric encryption ensures confidentiality and privacy by rendering data unreadable without the corresponding decryption key, thus protecting sensitive information from unauthorized access or interception.

However, symmetric encryption requires secure key exchange mechanisms to distribute shared secret keys securely between communicating parties, which can be challenging to manage, particularly in large-scale or distributed systems. Key management techniques, including key exchange protocols, key generation algorithms, and key rotation policies, are essential for securely generating, distributing, and revoking symmetric encryption keys. For example, the Diffie-Hellman key exchange protocol enables secure negotiation of a shared secret key between two parties over an insecure communication channel, without pre-shared keys or secure key distribution mechanisms. By implementing robust key management practices, organizations can mitigate the risk of unauthorized access to symmetric encryption keys and protect their encrypted data and communications from interception or decryption by malicious actors.

On the other hand, asymmetric encryption, also known as public-key encryption, employs a pair of mathematically related keys – a public key and a private key – for encryption and decryption processes. The openssl command can be used to generate asymmetric encryption key pairs, such as RSA or Elliptic Curve Cryptography (ECC), and encrypt plaintext data using the recipient's public key and an encryption algorithm. For instance, the command "openssl rsautl -encrypt -in plaintext.txt -out ciphertext.enc -pubin -inkey recipient_public_key.pem" encrypts a file named plaintext.txt using RSA encryption with the recipient's public key stored in a file named recipient_public_key.pem, and stores the encrypted data in a file named ciphertext.enc. Asymmetric encryption provides stronger security guarantees and eliminates the need for secure key exchange mechanisms.

Moreover, asymmetric encryption offers additional security benefits, including digital signatures and key authentication, which can be used to verify the integrity and authenticity of encrypted data and the identity of communicating parties. Digital signatures, generated using the sender's private key and verified using the sender's public key, provide cryptographic proof of data integrity and authenticity. The openssl command can be utilized to generate digital signatures for files or messages using the sender's private key and verify the signatures using the sender's public key. By using digital signatures, organizations can ensure the integrity and authenticity of encrypted data and communications, protecting against data tampering or forgery by malicious actors.

Furthermore, asymmetric encryption facilitates secure key exchange mechanisms, such as key encapsulation, key agreement, and key transport protocols, which enable secure negotiation of symmetric encryption keys between communicating parties without pre-shared keys or secure key distribution mechanisms. For example, the Diffie-Hellman key exchange protocol securely negotiates a shared symmetric encryption key between two parties over an insecure communication channel using their respective public and private keys. By leveraging asymmetric encryption for key exchange, organizations can establish secure and confidential communications channels with external parties or untrusted networks, ensuring the confidentiality, integrity, and authenticity of encrypted data and communications.

In summary, symmetric and asymmetric encryption are fundamental cryptographic techniques used to secure data and communications in modern computer systems. Symmetric encryption is efficient for encrypting large volumes of data but requires secure key exchange mechanisms. In contrast, asymmetric encryption provides stronger security guarantees and eliminates the need for secure key exchange mechanisms. By understanding the strengths and weaknesses of symmetric and asymmetric encryption, organizations can choose appropriate cryptographic techniques and key management practices to protect their sensitive data and communications from unauthorized access or interception by malicious actors.

Digital signatures and certificates are essential components of modern cybersecurity, providing a means to verify the authenticity, integrity, and origin of digital documents, messages, and transactions. Digital signatures use cryptographic techniques to create a unique digital fingerprint, or hash, of a document or message, which is then encrypted using the sender's private key. This encrypted hash, along with the sender's public key, forms the digital signature, which can be verified by recipients using the sender's public key to ensure that the document or message has not been altered or tampered with since it was signed. The openssl command can be used to generate digital signatures for files or messages using the sender's private key and verify the signatures using the sender's public key. For example, the command "openssl dgst -sha256 -sign sender_private_key.pem -out signature.sha256 plaintext.txt" generates a digital signature for a file named plaintext.txt using the sender's private key stored in a file named sender_private_key.pem and stores the signature in a file named signature.sha256. By using digital signatures, organizations can ensure the integrity and authenticity of digital documents and communications, protecting against data tampering or forgery by malicious actors.

Moreover, digital certificates are cryptographic credentials that bind the identity of an entity, such as an individual, organization, or website, to a public key, allowing recipients to verify the authenticity and legitimacy of the entity's digital signature. Digital certificates are issued by trusted third-party entities called certificate authorities (CAs), which verify the identity of certificate applicants and digitally sign their public keys to create trusted certificates. Web browsers and operating systems come pre-installed with a list of trusted root CAs, whose digital signatures are used to verify the authenticity of certificates issued by intermediate CAs. The openssl command can be used to generate digital certificate signing requests (CSRs), which contain information about the entity requesting a certificate, including its public key. For example, the command "openssl req -new -key private_key.pem -out csr.pem" generates a CSR for a certificate using a private key stored in a file named private_key.pem and stores the CSR in a file named csr.pem. By using digital certificates, organizations can establish secure communications channels, authenticate users and devices, and verify the legitimacy of digital signatures, protecting against identity theft, impersonation, and man-in-the-middle attacks.

Furthermore, digital certificates are widely used in public key infrastructure (PKI) systems, which provide a framework for managing and distributing digital certificates and public keys securely. PKI systems include a hierarchy of CAs, including root CAs, intermediate CAs, and issuing CAs, which are responsible for issuing, revoking, and managing digital certificates. Certificate revocation lists (CRLs) and online certificate status protocol (OCSP) are used to check the validity and status of digital certificates, allowing users to verify whether a certificate has been revoked or expired before trusting it. The openssl command can be used to generate CRLs, which contain a list of revoked certificates issued by a CA, allowing users to check the status of certificates issued by that CA. For example, the command "openssl ca -gencrl -out crl.pem" generates a CRL for a CA and stores it in a file named crl.pem. By using PKI systems, organizations can establish trust relationships, authenticate users and devices, and secure digital transactions, ensuring the confidentiality, integrity, and authenticity of sensitive information and communications.

Additionally, digital certificates are widely used to secure communications over the internet, particularly in protocols such as HTTPS, which encrypts web traffic using the Transport Layer Security (TLS) protocol. TLS relies on digital certificates to authenticate web servers and establish secure connections with clients, ensuring that data transmitted between the client and server is encrypted and protected from eavesdropping or interception by malicious actors. The openssl command can be used to generate digital certificates for web servers and configure TLS settings to enable HTTPS connections. For example, the command "openssl req -new -x509 -days 365 -key private_key.pem -out certificate.pem" generates a self-signed digital certificate for a web server using a private key stored in a file named private_key.pem and stores the certificate in a file named certificate.pem. By using digital certificates and TLS, organizations can encrypt sensitive web traffic, authenticate web servers, and protect against man-in-the-middle attacks, ensuring the security and privacy of online communications and transactions.

Moreover, digital certificates are used to authenticate and secure email communications using protocols such as S/MIME (Secure/Multipurpose Internet Mail Extensions), which encrypts and signs email messages to protect them from interception and tampering by unauthorized parties. S/MIME relies on digital certificates to authenticate email senders and encrypt email messages using their public keys, ensuring that only authorized recipients can read and decrypt the messages. The openssl command can be used to generate digital certificates for email clients and configure S/MIME settings to enable email encryption and signing. For example, the command "openssl req -new -key private_key.pem -out csr.pem" generates a CSR for an email client using a private key stored in a file named private_key.pem and stores the CSR in a file named csr.pem. By using digital certificates and

S/MIME, organizations can protect sensitive email communications, authenticate email senders, and prevent unauthorized access to confidential information, ensuring the security and privacy of electronic correspondence.

In summary, digital signatures and certificates are essential components of modern cybersecurity, providing organizations with the means to verify the authenticity, integrity, and origin of digital documents, messages, and transactions. By using digital signatures and certificates, organizations can ensure the security and trustworthiness of their communications channels, authenticate users and devices, and protect against identity theft, impersonation, and data tampering. Moreover, digital certificates play a crucial role in securing communications over the internet, enabling secure connections between clients and servers, encrypting sensitive web traffic, and protecting against man-in-the-middle attacks. Additionally, digital certificates are used to authenticate and secure email communications, ensuring the confidentiality, integrity, and authenticity of electronic correspondence. By understanding the principles and techniques of digital signatures and certificates, organizations can establish secure and reliable communications channels, protect sensitive information, and maintain the confidentiality, integrity, and authenticity of digital assets.

Chapter 4: Fundamentals of Access Control Systems

Access Control Lists (ACLs) are essential security mechanisms used in computer systems and networks to regulate access to resources, files, directories, and services based on predefined rules and policies. ACLs are commonly implemented in operating systems, network devices, and applications to enforce security policies and restrict user access to authorized entities. In Unix-based operating systems such as Linux, ACLs can be managed using the "setfacl" command, which allows users to set permissions for specific users or groups on files and directories. For example, the command "setfacl -m u:username:rw file.txt" grants read and write permissions to a user named "username" on a file named "file.txt." By using ACLs, administrators can define granular access controls and restrict access to sensitive data or resources, ensuring that only authorized users or groups can access or modify them. Additionally, ACLs can be used to implement role-based access control (RBAC) policies, which assign permissions to users based on their roles or responsibilities within an organization. For example, the command "setfacl -m g:admin:rw directory" grants read and write permissions to a group named "admin" on a directory, allowing members of the "admin" group to manage the contents of the directory. By using RBAC policies and ACLs, organizations can streamline access management processes, reduce the risk of unauthorized access, and enforce security policies consistently across their systems and networks.

Moreover, ACLs are commonly used in network devices such as routers, switches, and firewalls to control access to network resources and services based on IP addresses, port numbers, or protocols. In Cisco IOS devices, ACLs can be configured using the "access-list" command, which allows administrators to define access control rules and apply them to specific interfaces or traffic flows. For example, the command "access-list 101 permit tcp any host 192.168.1.1 eq 22" permits TCP traffic from any source IP address to a destination IP address "192.168.1.1" on port 22 (SSH). By configuring ACLs on network devices, administrators can restrict access to network resources, filter incoming and outgoing traffic, and protect against unauthorized access attempts or network-based attacks. Additionally, ACLs can be used in conjunction with other security mechanisms such as intrusion detection and prevention systems (IDPS) to provide layered defenses and enhance overall network security posture.

Furthermore, ACLs are widely used in web servers and applications to control access to web resources, directories, and APIs based on user roles, permissions, or authentication status. In Apache HTTP Server, ACLs can be configured using the "Require" directive in the server configuration files, which allows administrators to specify access control rules based on various criteria such as user authentication, IP addresses, or HTTP request methods. For example, the directive "Require ip 192.168.1.0/24" restricts access to a directory or web resource to clients with IP addresses in the range "192.168.1.0/24." By using ACLs in web servers and applications, administrators can enforce access control policies, protect sensitive data, and prevent unauthorized access to web resources or APIs. Additionally, ACLs can be integrated with authentication mechanisms such as LDAP (Lightweight Directory Access Protocol) or OAuth (Open Authorization) to provide fine-grained access control based on user identities or attributes, ensuring that only authenticated and authorized users can access protected resources.

Moreover, ACLs are used in database management systems (DBMS) to control access to database objects such as tables, views, and stored procedures based on user privileges or roles. In MySQL, ACLs can be managed using the "GRANT" and "REVOKE" statements, which allow database administrators to grant or revoke privileges on database objects to specific users or roles. For example, the statement "GRANT SELECT ON table_name TO user_name" grants the SELECT privilege on a table named "table_name" to a user named "user_name." By using ACLs in DBMS, administrators can enforce data security policies, restrict access to sensitive data, and prevent unauthorized modification or deletion of database objects. Additionally, ACLs can be used in conjunction with database auditing and logging mechanisms to track access to sensitive data, monitor user activities, and detect potential security breaches or insider threats.

Furthermore, ACLs are essential in cloud computing environments to control access to cloud resources, virtual machines, and storage objects based on user identities, roles, or policies. In cloud platforms such as Amazon Web Services (AWS) or Microsoft Azure, ACLs can be configured using Identity and Access Management (IAM) policies, which allow administrators to define access control rules and permissions for specific users, groups, or roles. For example, IAM policies in AWS can be used to grant or deny access to AWS resources such as S3 buckets, EC2 instances, or RDS databases based on various criteria such as user attributes, IP addresses, or time-based conditions. By using ACLs in cloud environments, organizations can ensure data security, compliance, and governance, and prevent unauthorized access to sensitive cloud resources or data. Additionally, ACLs can be integrated with cloud security services such as AWS Security Groups or Azure Network Security Groups to provide network-level access control and firewalling capabilities, ensuring that only authorized traffic is allowed to access cloud resources.

In summary, Access Control Lists (ACLs) are essential security mechanisms used in computer systems, networks, applications, and cloud environments to regulate access to resources, files, directories, and services based on predefined rules and policies. By using ACLs, organizations can enforce access control policies, restrict user access to authorized entities, and protect against unauthorized access or data breaches. Moreover, ACLs can be configured and managed using CLI commands or configuration files, allowing administrators to define granular access controls and enforce security policies consistently across various systems and environments. By understanding the principles and techniques of ACLs, organizations can enhance their security posture, mitigate the risk of unauthorized access, and protect sensitive data and resources from potential security threats or breaches.

Authentication methods and mechanisms play a critical role in ensuring the security of computer systems, networks, and applications by verifying the identities of users and devices and granting access only to authorized entities. Authentication is the process of validating the identity of a user or device based on credentials such as usernames, passwords, biometric data, cryptographic keys, or digital certificates. The authentication process typically involves three main factors: something the user knows (such as a password or PIN), something the user has (such as a smart card or token), and something the user is (such as biometric data like fingerprints or iris scans). Multi-factor authentication (MFA) combines two or more of these factors to enhance security and reduce the risk of unauthorized access. In Unix-based operating systems, authentication mechanisms can be configured using the "passwd" command, which allows users to set or change their passwords, and the "pam" (Pluggable Authentication Modules) framework, which provides a flexible mechanism for authentication and access control. For example, the command "passwd" allows users to change their passwords, while the "pam_unix" module in the "/etc/pam.d/" directory can be configured to enforce password policies such as minimum length, complexity, and expiration. By using MFA and strong password policies, organizations can enhance the security of their systems and prevent unauthorized access by malicious actors.

Moreover, biometric authentication methods, such as fingerprint recognition, facial recognition, iris scans, and voice recognition, are increasingly being used to verify the identities of users and enhance security. Biometric authentication relies on unique physiological or behavioral characteristics of individuals to authenticate their identities, providing a more secure and convenient alternative to traditional password-based authentication. Biometric authentication systems capture biometric data from users, such as fingerprints or facial features, and compare it against stored templates to verify their identities. In Windows operating systems, biometric authentication can be configured using the "Windows Hello" feature, which allows users to log in to their devices using facial recognition, fingerprint scans, or iris scans. For example, users can enroll their biometric data in the "Windows Hello" settings and use it to unlock their devices instead of entering a password. By using biometric authentication, organizations can improve the user experience, enhance security, and reduce the risk of unauthorized access or identity theft.

Furthermore, cryptographic authentication methods, such as digital signatures and certificates, are used to authenticate the identities of users, devices, and applications in secure communications and transactions. Digital signatures use cryptographic techniques to create a unique digital fingerprint, or hash, of a message or document, which is then encrypted using the sender's private key. The recipient can verify the digital signature using the sender's public key to ensure the integrity and authenticity of the message or document. In SSL/TLS (Secure Sockets Layer/Transport Layer Security) protocols, cryptographic authentication is used to authenticate web servers and establish secure connections with clients. For example, web servers present digital certificates signed by trusted certificate authorities (CAs) to prove their identities to clients, ensuring that clients are communicating with legitimate servers and not impostors. By using cryptographic authentication, organizations can secure their communications, protect against eavesdropping and tampering, and establish trust relationships with external parties.

Additionally, token-based authentication methods, such as smart cards, security tokens, and one-time passwords (OTPs), are used to authenticate users and devices in secure access control systems. Tokens are physical or virtual devices that generate unique authentication codes or credentials that users can use to authenticate their identities. In two-factor authentication (2FA) systems, users typically enter a password or PIN (something they know) along with a one-time authentication code generated by a token (something they have) to access secure systems or services. In VPN (Virtual Private Network) configurations, token-based authentication can be configured using the "OpenVPN" software, which supports various authentication methods, including certificates, usernames/passwords, and OTPs. For example, users can generate OTPs using mobile apps or hardware tokens and enter them along with their usernames/passwords to authenticate their VPN connections. By using token-based authentication, organizations can strengthen access controls, mitigate the risk of password-based attacks, and enhance the security of their systems and networks.

Moreover, federated authentication methods, such as OAuth (Open Authorization) and OpenID Connect, are used to authenticate users across multiple systems, applications, and domains using a single set of credentials. Federated authentication allows users to log in to different services and applications using their existing accounts from identity providers (IdPs) such as Google, Facebook, or Microsoft. In OAuth-based authentication, users authorize third-party applications to access their resources or perform actions on their behalf without sharing their credentials directly. In OpenID Connect, users authenticate to an identity provider (IdP) using their credentials, and the IdP issues tokens that can be used to authenticate users to other services or applications. For example, users can log in to a website using their Google or Facebook accounts instead of creating new accounts, reducing friction and improving the user experience. By using federated authentication, organizations can simplify access management, streamline user authentication processes, and enhance the interoperability of their systems and applications.

In summary, authentication methods and mechanisms are essential components of cybersecurity, enabling organizations to verify the identities of users, devices, and applications and grant access only to authorized entities. By using a combination of authentication factors, including passwords, biometrics, tokens, and cryptographic credentials, organizations can strengthen access controls, enhance security, and prevent unauthorized access or identity theft. Moreover, authentication technologies such as MFA, biometric authentication, cryptographic authentication, token-based authentication, and federated authentication provide organizations with flexible and scalable solutions to meet their security requirements and compliance obligations. By understanding the principles and techniques of authentication, organizations can implement robust authentication mechanisms, protect against security threats, and safeguard their sensitive data and resources from unauthorized access or misuse.

Chapter 5: Introduction to Security Models and Frameworks

Security models are conceptual frameworks that define the mechanisms and policies used to enforce security controls and protect computer systems, networks, and data from unauthorized access, disclosure, modification, or destruction. These models provide a structured approach to designing, implementing, and managing security measures based on established principles, standards, and best practices. Several common security models are widely used in the field of cybersecurity, each offering unique features, advantages, and limitations. The Bell-LaPadula model, for example, is a formal security model used to enforce mandatory access controls (MAC) based on the principles of confidentiality and integrity. The model defines a set of rules and policies that govern the flow of information between subjects (users or processes) and objects (resources or data) in a computer system. In the Bell-LaPadula model, access permissions are determined by security labels assigned to subjects and objects, such as classification levels (e.g., top secret, secret, confidential, unclassified) and security categories (e.g., read, write, execute). To enforce the Bell-LaPadula model, administrators can use access control mechanisms such as discretionary access control lists (ACLs) or role-based access control (RBAC) policies to restrict access to sensitive data based on the security labels assigned to users and resources.

Another common security model is the Biba model, which is designed to enforce integrity controls and prevent unauthorized modification or corruption of data. The Biba model is based on the principle of integrity and defines a set of rules and policies that govern the flow of information between subjects and objects in a computer system. In the Biba model, access permissions are determined by security labels assigned to subjects and objects, such as integrity levels (e.g., low, medium, high) and integrity categories (e.g., read, write, execute). To enforce the Biba model, administrators can use access control mechanisms such as mandatory access control (MAC) policies or integrity verification mechanisms to prevent users from accessing or modifying data beyond their authorized integrity levels.

Additionally, the Clark-Wilson model is a security model used to enforce integrity controls and ensure the consistency and correctness of data and transactions in a computer system. The Clark-Wilson model is based on the principles of well-formed transactions and separation of duties and defines a set of rules and policies that govern the creation, modification, and validation of data and transactions. In the Clark-Wilson model, access permissions are determined by rules and constraints defined in a security policy, such as access control lists (ACLs), transaction logs, and audit trails. To enforce the Clark-Wilson model, administrators can use access control mechanisms such as role-based access control (RBAC) policies, data validation rules, and transaction processing mechanisms to ensure the integrity and consistency of data and transactions.

Furthermore, the Brewer-Nash model, also known as the Brewer-Nash theorem or the CAP theorem, is a theoretical framework used to analyze the trade-offs between consistency, availability, and partition tolerance in distributed computer systems. The CAP theorem states that it is impossible for a distributed computer system to simultaneously guarantee consistency (all nodes see the same data at the same time), availability (every request receives a response, even in the presence of failures), and partition tolerance (the system continues to operate despite network partitions) in the event of network partitions or failures. To address this challenge, administrators can use replication techniques, such as multi-master replication or eventual consistency, to balance consistency, availability, and partition tolerance based on the requirements and priorities of the system.

Moreover, the Non-Interference model is a security model used to enforce confidentiality controls and prevent information leakage or unauthorized disclosure of sensitive data. The Non-Interference model is based on the principle of non-interference, which states that the actions of low-level users should not interfere with the actions or observations of high-level users. In the Non-Interference model, access permissions are determined by security labels assigned to subjects and objects, such as security levels (e.g., low, medium, high) and security categories (e.g., read, write, execute). To enforce the Non-Interference model, administrators can use access control mechanisms such as mandatory access control (MAC) policies or data isolation techniques to prevent users from accessing or disclosing sensitive information beyond their authorized security levels.

Furthermore, the Common Criteria (CC) is an international standard used to evaluate and certify the security features and capabilities of IT products and systems. The Common Criteria defines a set of requirements and criteria that IT products and systems must meet to achieve different levels of security assurance, such as EAL (Evaluation Assurance Level) ratings. To comply with the Common Criteria, vendors and developers must undergo a rigorous evaluation process conducted by accredited testing laboratories, which assesses the security functions, mechanisms, and controls implemented in their products and systems. By achieving Common Criteria certification, vendors and developers can demonstrate the security and reliability of their products and systems to customers, partners, and regulatory authorities.

In summary, security models are essential tools used in cybersecurity to enforce security controls, protect sensitive data, and mitigate the risk of unauthorized access or disclosure. By understanding the principles and features of common security models such as the Bell-LaPadula model, Biba model, Clark-Wilson model, Brewer-Nash model, Non-Interference model, and Common Criteria, organizations can design, implement, and manage robust security architectures that meet their specific requirements and objectives. Additionally, by using access control mechanisms, encryption techniques, authentication methods, and other security controls, organizations can enhance the security of their systems and networks and safeguard their sensitive information and resources from potential security threats and vulnerabilities.

Implementing security frameworks in practice involves the deployment of structured methodologies, policies, and controls to protect computer systems, networks, and data from potential security threats and vulnerabilities. Security frameworks provide organizations with a systematic approach to identifying, assessing, and managing security risks, as well as establishing controls and safeguards to mitigate those risks effectively. Several security frameworks are widely used in the field of cybersecurity, each offering guidance and best practices for implementing comprehensive security programs tailored to specific industries, regulatory requirements, and organizational needs. One such framework is the NIST Cybersecurity Framework (CSF), developed by the National Institute of Standards and Technology (NIST) to help organizations manage and reduce cybersecurity risks. The NIST CSF is based on five core functions: Identify, Protect, Detect, Respond, and Recover, which provide a structured approach to managing cybersecurity risk across an organization. To implement the NIST CSF, organizations can use the framework's guidelines and recommendations to assess their current cybersecurity posture, identify gaps and weaknesses, and develop a roadmap for improving their security capabilities. For example, organizations can use the "Identify" function to inventory and classify their assets, assess their cybersecurity risks, and prioritize their security initiatives based on their criticality and impact. By using the NIST CSF, organizations can align their security efforts with industry best practices, regulatory requirements, and emerging threats, enhancing their resilience to cybersecurity incidents and breaches.

Another widely used security framework is the ISO/IEC 27001 standard, which provides a systematic approach to implementing an Information Security Management System (ISMS) to protect the confidentiality, integrity, and availability of information assets. The ISO/IEC 27001 standard is based on a risk-based approach to information security management, which involves identifying, assessing, and treating security risks to achieve acceptable levels of risk. To implement ISO/IEC 27001, organizations can follow a structured methodology that includes the following steps: conducting a risk assessment to identify and prioritize security risks, defining security objectives and controls to mitigate those risks, implementing and operating the controls effectively, and monitoring and reviewing the effectiveness of the ISMS regularly. For example, organizations can use the "Control Objectives for Information and Related Technologies" (COBIT) framework to define control objectives and requirements for specific information security domains, such as access control, cryptography, and incident management. By using the ISO/IEC 27001 standard, organizations can establish a robust framework for managing information security risks, achieving compliance with regulatory requirements, and demonstrating their commitment to protecting sensitive information and data assets.

Moreover, the Payment Card Industry Data Security Standard (PCI DSS) is a security framework developed by the Payment Card Industry Security Standards Council (PCI SSC) to protect payment card data and ensure the security of cardholder information. The PCI DSS provides a set of requirements and best practices for securing payment card transactions, including the use of encryption, access controls, network segmentation, and regular security testing and monitoring. To comply with the PCI DSS, organizations that handle payment card data must implement and maintain a secure network, protect cardholder data, maintain a vulnerability management program, implement strong access control measures, regularly monitor and test their networks, and maintain an information security policy. For example, organizations can use the "Payment Card Industry Data Security Standard Self-Assessment Questionnaire" (PCI DSS SAQ) to assess their compliance with the standard and identify areas for improvement. By implementing the PCI DSS, organizations can protect sensitive payment card data, reduce the risk of data breaches and fraud, and maintain the trust and confidence of customers and partners.

Furthermore, the Health Insurance Portability and Accountability Act (HIPAA) Security Rule is a security framework developed by the U.S. Department of Health and Human Services (HHS) to protect the confidentiality, integrity, and availability of protected health information (PHI). The HIPAA Security Rule establishes requirements for covered entities and their business associates to implement administrative, physical, and technical safeguards to protect PHI from unauthorized access, disclosure, or use. To comply with the HIPAA Security Rule, organizations must conduct a risk analysis to identify and assess security risks to PHI, implement security measures to mitigate those risks, and maintain ongoing compliance through regular monitoring and auditing. For example, organizations can use encryption to protect PHI in transit and at rest, implement access controls to restrict access to PHI based on the principle of least privilege, and establish procedures for responding to and reporting security incidents and breaches. By implementing the HIPAA Security Rule, covered entities can protect the privacy and security of patient information, comply with regulatory requirements, and avoid costly penalties and sanctions for non-compliance.

Moreover, the General Data Protection Regulation (GDPR) is a comprehensive data protection framework developed by the European Union (EU) to regulate the processing of personal data and protect the privacy rights of EU residents. The GDPR establishes requirements for organizations to implement appropriate technical and organizational measures to ensure the security of personal data and protect it from unauthorized access, disclosure, or loss. To comply with the GDPR, organizations must implement security measures such as encryption, pseudonymization, access controls, and data minimization to protect personal data from unauthorized access or disclosure. For example, organizations can use encryption to protect personal data in transit and at rest, implement access controls to restrict access to personal data based on the principle of least privilege, and conduct regular security assessments and audits to ensure compliance with the GDPR's security requirements. By implementing the GDPR, organizations can demonstrate their commitment to protecting the privacy rights of individuals, comply with regulatory requirements, and avoid fines and penalties for non-compliance.

In summary, implementing security frameworks in practice requires organizations to adopt a systematic approach to managing cybersecurity risks and protecting sensitive information assets. By following established methodologies, guidelines, and best practices provided by security frameworks such as the NIST CSF, ISO/IEC 27001, PCI DSS, HIPAA Security Rule, and GDPR, organizations can establish robust security programs tailored to their specific requirements and objectives. By implementing effective security controls, monitoring and responding to security incidents, and maintaining ongoing compliance with regulatory requirements, organizations can enhance their resilience to cybersecurity threats and breaches, protect sensitive data and information assets, and maintain the trust and confidence of customers, partners, and stakeholders.

Chapter 6: Principles of Secure Software Development

Secure coding practices are essential guidelines and techniques used by software developers to write code that is resilient to security vulnerabilities and threats, reducing the risk of exploitation and compromise. These practices encompass various principles, methodologies, and best practices aimed at addressing common security vulnerabilities and weaknesses in software applications. One such practice is input validation, which involves validating and sanitizing user input to prevent injection attacks such as SQL injection, cross-site scripting (XSS), and command injection. Developers can use libraries and frameworks that provide built-in input validation mechanisms or implement custom validation logic to ensure that user input meets expected criteria and does not contain malicious or unexpected characters. For example, in web applications, developers can use server-side validation frameworks such as Spring Validation in Java or Express Validator in Node.js to validate user input before processing it further, reducing the risk of injection attacks. By implementing input validation, developers can prevent attackers from exploiting vulnerabilities in their code and manipulating user input to execute malicious commands or scripts.

Another important secure coding practice is output encoding, which involves encoding and escaping user-generated content to prevent XSS attacks and other forms of code injection. Output encoding ensures that user input is displayed or rendered correctly in web browsers without executing any embedded scripts or malicious code. Developers can use encoding functions provided by programming languages or libraries, such as htmlspecialchars() in PHP or encodeURI() in JavaScript, to encode user input before displaying it in web pages or rendering it in HTML, CSS, or JavaScript contexts. For example, developers can use output encoding techniques to sanitize user-generated content in web forms, comment sections, or chat applications, reducing the risk of XSS attacks and protecting users from malicious scripts injected into web pages. By incorporating output encoding into their code, developers can mitigate the risk of code injection vulnerabilities and protect users from potential security threats and attacks.

Furthermore, secure authentication and session management are critical aspects of secure coding practices, ensuring that users are authenticated and authorized to access protected resources and data. Developers should use strong authentication mechanisms such as multi-factor authentication (MFA), password hashing, and session management techniques to verify the identities of users and protect their credentials from unauthorized access or disclosure. For example, developers can use libraries and frameworks such as Passport.js in Node.js or Spring Security in Java to implement authentication and session management features in web applications, allowing users to log in securely and access their accounts without compromising their credentials. By implementing secure authentication and session management practices, developers can prevent unauthorized access to sensitive data and resources, protect user privacy, and comply with regulatory requirements such as the General Data Protection Regulation (GDPR) and the Health Insurance Portability and Accountability Act (HIPAA).

Additionally, secure error handling is an essential aspect of secure coding practices, ensuring that errors and exceptions are handled gracefully and securely to prevent information leakage and potential security vulnerabilities. Developers should avoid exposing sensitive information such as stack traces, error messages, or system details in error responses or logs, as this information can be exploited by attackers to gain insight into the internal workings of the application and identify potential security weaknesses. Instead, developers should use generic error messages and log messages that do not reveal sensitive information and provide users with clear and informative feedback without disclosing internal system details. For example, developers can use logging frameworks such as Log4j in Java or Winston in Node.js to log error messages and exceptions securely, ensuring that sensitive information is not exposed to potential attackers. By implementing secure error handling practices, developers can reduce the risk of information disclosure and protect the confidentiality and integrity of sensitive data and system resources.

Moreover, secure data storage and transmission are essential aspects of secure coding practices, ensuring that sensitive data is encrypted and protected from unauthorized access or interception during storage and transmission. Developers should use strong encryption algorithms and protocols such as AES (Advanced Encryption Standard) or TLS (Transport Layer Security) to encrypt sensitive data before storing it in databases or transmitting it over insecure networks. For example, developers can use encryption libraries such as bcrypt in Node.js or Java Cryptography Extension (JCE) in Java to encrypt passwords and other sensitive data before storing them in databases, reducing the risk of data breaches and unauthorized access. Similarly, developers can use HTTPS (HTTP Secure) protocol to encrypt data transmitted between clients and servers, ensuring that sensitive information such as login credentials, payment details, and personal information is protected from eavesdropping and interception by malicious actors. By implementing secure data storage and transmission practices, developers can protect sensitive information from unauthorized access, maintain data confidentiality and integrity, and comply with regulatory requirements such as the Payment Card Industry Data Security Standard (PCI DSS) and the European Union's General Data Protection Regulation (GDPR).

In summary, secure coding practices are essential for developing secure and resilient software applications that can withstand potential security threats and attacks. By incorporating input validation, output encoding, secure authentication and session management, secure error handling, and secure data storage and transmission into their code, developers can reduce the risk of security vulnerabilities and protect users from potential security threats and breaches. Moreover, by following established guidelines and best practices provided by security standards such as the Open Web Application Security Project (OWASP) Top 10, the SANS Institute's Secure Coding Practices, and the CERT Secure Coding Standards, developers can ensure that their code is robust, reliable, and secure, and that it meets industry best practices and compliance requirements. By adopting secure coding practices, developers can contribute to building a more secure and trustworthy digital ecosystem, protecting users' privacy and data security, and enhancing the resilience of software applications against emerging security threats and vulnerabilities.

Software Development Lifecycle (SDLC) security considerations are vital aspects of developing secure and resilient software applications that can withstand potential security threats and vulnerabilities throughout the development process. The SDLC encompasses various phases, methodologies, and practices aimed at designing, implementing, testing, deploying, and maintaining software applications in a systematic and structured manner. Security considerations should be integrated into each phase of the SDLC to ensure that security requirements are identified, addressed, and validated throughout the software development process. One important aspect of SDLC security considerations is threat modeling, which involves identifying and analyzing potential security threats and vulnerabilities that could affect the confidentiality, integrity, and availability of the software application. Developers can use threat modeling techniques such as STRIDE (Spoofing, Tampering, Repudiation, Information Disclosure, Denial of Service, Elevation of Privilege) or DREAD (Damage, Reproducibility, Exploitability, Affected Users, Discoverability) to identify and prioritize security threats based on their severity and impact on the application. For example, developers can use threat modeling tools such as Microsoft Threat Modeling Tool or OWASP Threat Dragon to create threat models that identify potential security risks and suggest mitigations to address them.

Another important aspect of SDLC security considerations is secure coding practices, which involve following established guidelines and best practices to write code that is resilient to security vulnerabilities and threats. Secure coding practices include input validation, output encoding, authentication and session management, error handling, and data storage and transmission security. Developers can use code analysis tools such as static analysis tools or code review processes to identify potential security vulnerabilities in their code and address them before deploying the application. For example, developers can use static analysis tools such as SonarQube or Veracode to scan their code for common security vulnerabilities such as buffer overflows, SQL injection, cross-site scripting (XSS), and insecure cryptographic algorithms, and fix them before releasing the application to production.

Moreover, secure configuration management is an essential aspect of SDLC security considerations, ensuring that software components and configurations are securely configured and maintained throughout their lifecycle. Developers should follow secure configuration guidelines provided by industry standards such as the Center for Internet Security (CIS) benchmarks or vendor-specific security guides to configure software components, platforms, and infrastructure securely. For example, developers can use configuration management tools such as Ansible, Puppet, or Chef to automate the deployment and configuration of software components and ensure that they are hardened and compliant with security best practices. By following secure configuration management practices, developers can reduce the attack surface of their applications, minimize the risk of security misconfigurations, and improve the overall security posture of their software environments.

Furthermore, secure testing and validation are critical aspects of SDLC security considerations, ensuring that software applications are thoroughly tested for security vulnerabilities and weaknesses before being deployed to production. Developers should conduct various types of security testing, including static analysis, dynamic analysis, penetration testing, and security code reviews, to identify and mitigate potential security risks. For example, developers can use dynamic analysis tools such as OWASP ZAP or Burp Suite to simulate real-world attacks and identify security vulnerabilities such as SQL injection, cross-site scripting (XSS), or broken authentication and session management. Additionally, developers can use penetration testing techniques to identify and exploit security vulnerabilities in their applications and infrastructure and validate the effectiveness of their security controls and mitigations. By conducting comprehensive security testing and validation, developers can identify and mitigate security vulnerabilities early in the development process, reducing the risk of security breaches and ensuring the reliability and security of their software applications.

Moreover, secure deployment and monitoring are essential aspects of SDLC security considerations, ensuring that software applications are deployed securely and monitored for potential security threats and vulnerabilities in production environments. Developers should use secure deployment practices such as automation, least privilege, and segregation of duties to deploy software applications securely and minimize the risk of unauthorized access or exploitation. For example, developers can use deployment automation tools such as Jenkins, Ansible, or Terraform to automate the deployment of software applications and infrastructure and ensure that security configurations are applied consistently across all environments. Additionally, developers should implement robust monitoring and logging mechanisms to monitor the behavior and performance of software applications in production and detect potential security incidents or anomalies. By monitoring system logs, network traffic, and user activities, developers can identify and respond to security incidents promptly, mitigate the impact of security breaches, and improve the overall security posture of their software environments.

In summary, SDLC security considerations are essential for developing secure and resilient software applications that can withstand potential security threats and vulnerabilities throughout the development process. By integrating security considerations into each phase of the SDLC, developers can identify, address, and validate security requirements effectively and ensure that software applications are designed, implemented, tested, deployed, and maintained securely. Moreover, by following established security best practices and guidelines, such as threat modeling, secure coding practices, secure configuration management, secure testing and validation, secure deployment and monitoring, developers can improve the security posture of their software applications, protect sensitive data and resources, and build trust and confidence with users, customers, and stakeholders.

Chapter 7: Exploring Physical Security Measures

Perimeter security solutions play a critical role in protecting organizations' networks, systems, and data from unauthorized access and cyber threats by establishing a secure boundary between internal and external networks. These solutions encompass various technologies, strategies, and best practices aimed at securing the network perimeter and preventing unauthorized access to sensitive resources and data. One key component of perimeter security solutions is the implementation of firewalls, which are network security devices that monitor and control incoming and outgoing traffic based on predetermined security rules. Firewalls can be deployed as hardware appliances, software applications, or virtual appliances and are configured to inspect network packets and enforce access policies to allow or deny traffic based on factors such as IP addresses, port numbers, and protocols. For example, organizations can use the iptables command in Linux to configure firewall rules and policies to restrict inbound and outbound traffic based on specific criteria, such as allowing only authorized IP addresses to access certain services or blocking traffic from known malicious IP addresses.

Additionally, intrusion detection and prevention systems (IDPS) are essential components of perimeter security solutions, designed to detect and block malicious activities and attacks targeting the network perimeter. IDPS solutions monitor network traffic and analyze it for signs of suspicious or malicious behavior, such as unauthorized access attempts, malware infections, or denial-of-service (DoS) attacks. When anomalous activity is detected, IDPS solutions can take proactive measures to block or mitigate the threat, such as blocking the source IP address, dropping malicious packets, or alerting security administrators. For example, organizations can deploy open-source IDPS solutions such as Snort or Suricata, which use signature-based detection, anomaly-based detection, or behavioral analysis techniques to detect and prevent a wide range of cyber threats and attacks targeting the network perimeter. By deploying IDPS solutions, organizations can enhance their ability to detect and respond to security incidents in real-time, reducing the risk of data breaches and network compromises.

Moreover, virtual private networks (VPNs) are commonly used in perimeter security solutions to establish secure and encrypted connections between remote users or branch offices and the corporate network. VPNs enable remote users to access corporate resources securely over the internet, protecting sensitive data and communications from interception or eavesdropping by unauthorized parties. VPNs use encryption protocols such as IPsec (Internet Protocol Security) or SSL/TLS (Secure Sockets Layer/Transport Layer Security) to encrypt network traffic and ensure confidentiality and integrity. For example, organizations can deploy VPN concentrators or gateways to provide secure remote access to corporate networks, allowing remote users to establish encrypted tunnels and authenticate themselves using username and password credentials or digital certificates. By implementing VPNs, organizations can extend their perimeter security controls to remote and mobile users, ensuring secure access to corporate resources from anywhere, at any time.

Furthermore, web application firewalls (WAFs) are essential components of perimeter security solutions, designed to protect web applications and APIs from common security threats and vulnerabilities, such as SQL injection, cross-site scripting (XSS), and cross-site request forgery (CSRF). WAFs sit between the web application and the internet, inspecting incoming HTTP requests and responses for malicious payloads or patterns and blocking or mitigating attacks in real-time. WAFs use various techniques such as signature-based detection, anomaly-based detection, and behavioral analysis to identify and block malicious traffic before it reaches the web application. For example, organizations can deploy cloud-based WAF services such as AWS WAF or Azure WAF to protect their web applications hosted on public cloud platforms, configuring custom rules and policies to filter and block malicious traffic based on specific criteria. By deploying WAFs, organizations can strengthen their perimeter defenses, protect web applications from common security threats, and comply with regulatory requirements such as the Payment Card Industry Data Security Standard (PCI DSS) and the General Data Protection Regulation (GDPR).

Additionally, email security gateways are critical components of perimeter security solutions, designed to protect organizations' email infrastructure from spam, phishing, malware, and other email-borne threats. Email security gateways inspect incoming and outgoing email traffic, filtering out malicious content, attachments, or links before they reach users' mailboxes. These solutions use various techniques such as content filtering, malware detection, URL filtering, and sender reputation analysis to identify and block malicious emails and prevent them from reaching users. For example, organizations can deploy on-premises email security gateways such as Cisco Email Security Appliance or cloud-based email security services such as Microsoft Exchange Online Protection to protect their email infrastructure from a wide range of email-borne threats. By deploying email security gateways, organizations can reduce the risk of email-based attacks, protect sensitive information, and maintain the integrity and availability of their email communications.

In summary, perimeter security solutions are essential components of organizations' cybersecurity posture, providing critical defenses against external threats and attacks targeting the network perimeter. By deploying technologies such as firewalls, intrusion detection and prevention systems, virtual private networks, web application firewalls, and email security gateways, organizations can establish secure boundaries around their networks, systems, and data, protecting them from unauthorized access, exploitation, and compromise. Additionally, by implementing best practices such as regular security assessments, vulnerability scanning, and security awareness training, organizations can enhance their ability to detect and respond to emerging threats and vulnerabilities, ensuring the resilience and integrity of their perimeter defenses.

Surveillance and monitoring technologies are critical components of modern security strategies, enabling organizations to monitor, analyze, and respond to security threats and incidents in real-time. These technologies encompass a wide range of tools, systems, and techniques designed to monitor physical and digital environments, collect relevant data and information, and provide insights into potential security risks and vulnerabilities. One key aspect of surveillance and monitoring technologies is the use of closed-circuit television (CCTV) systems, which are commonly used to monitor and record activity in physical spaces such as buildings, campuses, and public areas. CCTV systems consist of cameras, recording devices, and monitoring stations that capture video footage of the surrounding environment and store it for later review or analysis. Organizations can deploy CCTV cameras strategically to monitor entrances, exits, hallways, parking lots, and other critical areas, deterring criminal activity, and providing evidence in the event of security incidents. For example, organizations can use the "ffmpeg" command-line tool to configure and manage CCTV cameras and recording devices, enabling them to capture and store high-quality video footage for surveillance purposes.

Additionally, access control systems are essential surveillance and monitoring technologies used to regulate and control access to physical spaces, assets, and resources within an organization. Access control systems consist of hardware devices such as card readers, biometric scanners, and electronic locks, as well as software platforms that manage access permissions and credentials. These systems enable organizations to restrict access to sensitive areas, track the movement of personnel and visitors, and enforce security policies and procedures effectively. For example, organizations can use the "ldapsearch" command-line tool to query an LDAP directory server for user authentication and authorization information, verifying users' identities and determining their access rights based on predefined policies and roles.

Moreover, network monitoring and intrusion detection systems (IDS) are essential surveillance and monitoring technologies used to monitor and analyze network traffic for signs of suspicious or malicious activity. Network monitoring systems capture and analyze network packets in real-time, identifying anomalies, patterns, and indicators of compromise that may indicate a security threat or intrusion. IDS solutions complement network monitoring systems by providing automated detection and alerting capabilities, enabling organizations to respond to security incidents promptly. For example, organizations can use the "tcpdump" command-line tool to capture and analyze network traffic in real-time, monitoring for signs of unauthorized access, data exfiltration, or malware infections. Additionally, organizations can deploy open-source IDS solutions such as Snort or Suricata, which use signature-based detection, anomaly-based detection, or behavioral analysis techniques to detect and prevent a wide range of cyber threats and attacks targeting the network perimeter.

Furthermore, endpoint security solutions are critical surveillance and monitoring technologies used to protect endpoints such as desktops, laptops, servers, and mobile devices from security threats and vulnerabilities. Endpoint security solutions consist of antivirus software, host-based intrusion detection systems (HIDS), endpoint detection and response (EDR) solutions, and other security tools designed to monitor, detect, and respond to security threats at the endpoint level. These solutions enable organizations to protect sensitive data and resources, enforce security policies, and prevent malware infections, ransomware attacks, and other cyber threats. For example, organizations can use the "clamscan" command-line tool to scan files and directories for malware infections on Linux-based endpoints, detecting and removing malicious files and applications that may compromise system security.

Moreover, security information and event management (SIEM) systems are essential surveillance and monitoring technologies used to aggregate, correlate, and analyze security events and logs from various sources within an organization's IT infrastructure. SIEM solutions collect log data from network devices, servers, applications, and security appliances, and analyze it for signs of security incidents, policy violations, or abnormal behavior. These solutions enable organizations to detect and respond to security threats in real-time, correlate events across multiple systems, and generate actionable insights to improve their security posture. For example, organizations can use the "syslog-ng" command-line tool to collect and forward syslog messages from network devices and servers to a centralized SIEM platform, enabling them to monitor and analyze security events and logs from a single console.

In summary, surveillance and monitoring technologies play a crucial role in modern security operations, enabling organizations to monitor, analyze, and respond to security threats and incidents effectively. By deploying CCTV systems, access control systems, network monitoring and IDS solutions, endpoint security solutions, and SIEM systems, organizations can establish comprehensive surveillance and monitoring capabilities, protect sensitive data and resources, and detect and mitigate security threats in real-time. Additionally, by leveraging command-line tools and open-source solutions, organizations can customize and optimize their surveillance and monitoring infrastructure to meet their specific security requirements and objectives, enhancing their ability to safeguard against emerging security threats and vulnerabilities.

Chapter 8: Fundamentals of Security Assessments and Audits

Vulnerability assessment techniques are critical processes used by organizations to identify, analyze, and prioritize security vulnerabilities in their IT infrastructure, applications, and systems. These techniques encompass various methodologies, tools, and practices aimed at assessing the security posture of an organization and identifying potential weaknesses that could be exploited by malicious actors. One common vulnerability assessment technique is the use of vulnerability scanning tools, which are automated software applications designed to scan IT systems and networks for known security vulnerabilities and misconfigurations. Vulnerability scanning tools conduct comprehensive scans of network devices, servers, applications, and databases, identifying vulnerabilities such as missing security patches, outdated software versions, weak passwords, and insecure configurations. For example, organizations can use the "Nmap" command-line tool to perform port scanning and version detection on network hosts, identifying open ports and services that may be vulnerable to exploitation by attackers.

Additionally, penetration testing, also known as ethical hacking, is a proactive vulnerability assessment technique used to simulate real-world cyber attacks and assess the security resilience of an organization's IT infrastructure and applications. Penetration testers, or ethical hackers, use a combination of manual and automated techniques to identify and exploit security vulnerabilities, demonstrating how attackers could potentially compromise systems and gain unauthorized access to sensitive data and resources. Penetration testing engagements typically involve four main phases: reconnaissance, scanning, exploitation, and post-exploitation. For example, organizations can use the "Metasploit" framework, a popular penetration testing tool, to simulate various types of cyber attacks such as remote code execution, SQL injection, and cross-site scripting (XSS), and assess their impact on target systems.

Moreover, vulnerability assessment techniques often include web application scanning, which focuses on identifying security vulnerabilities and weaknesses in web applications and APIs that could be exploited by attackers to compromise sensitive data or execute malicious actions. Web application scanning tools analyze web applications and APIs for common vulnerabilities such as SQL injection, cross-site scripting (XSS), cross-site request forgery (CSRF), and insecure authentication and authorization mechanisms. For example, organizations can use the "OWASP ZAP" (Zed Attack Proxy) tool to perform automated scans of web applications and APIs, identifying security vulnerabilities and generating detailed reports with recommendations for remediation.

Furthermore, configuration auditing is an essential vulnerability assessment technique used to evaluate the security configurations of IT systems, devices, and applications against established security standards and best practices. Configuration auditing tools examine system configurations, settings, and parameters to identify deviations from security policies and guidelines, such as weak password policies, unnecessary services and protocols, and insecure network configurations. For example, organizations can use the "OpenSCAP" (Security Content Automation Protocol) tool to perform automated configuration audits of Linux-based systems, checking for compliance with security benchmarks such as the Center for Internet Security (CIS) benchmarks or the Defense Information Systems Agency (DISA) Security Technical Implementation Guides (STIGs).

Additionally, vulnerability assessment techniques may include manual code review and static code analysis, which involve reviewing software source code and identifying potential security vulnerabilities and weaknesses that could be exploited by attackers. Manual code review involves reviewing software source code line by line to identify logic errors, buffer overflows, input validation vulnerabilities, and other security issues. Static code analysis tools automatically analyze software source code for common programming errors, security vulnerabilities, and coding best practices violations. For example, organizations can use the "grep" command-line tool to search for specific patterns and keywords in source code files, such as "TODO," "FIXME," or "security," to identify potential areas of concern that require further review or analysis.

Moreover, vulnerability assessment techniques often include database scanning and auditing, which focus on identifying security vulnerabilities and weaknesses in database systems and applications that could be exploited by attackers to access or manipulate sensitive data. Database scanning tools analyze database configurations, user permissions, and access controls to identify misconfigurations, weak passwords, and other security issues that could pose a risk to data confidentiality, integrity, and availability. For example, organizations can use the "sqlmap" command-line tool to perform automated SQL injection tests against web applications and APIs that interact with backend databases, identifying vulnerabilities that could be exploited to extract or modify sensitive data.

In summary, vulnerability assessment techniques are essential for organizations to identify, prioritize, and mitigate security vulnerabilities and weaknesses in their IT infrastructure, applications, and systems. By leveraging a combination of automated tools, manual techniques, and best practices, organizations can conduct comprehensive vulnerability assessments, assess their security posture, and take proactive measures to address potential risks and threats. Additionally, by integrating vulnerability assessment techniques into their security programs and processes, organizations can improve their overall security posture, reduce the risk of security breaches and data breaches, and enhance their ability to protect sensitive data and resources from exploitation by malicious actors.

Security audit planning and execution are critical processes within an organization's cybersecurity framework, aimed at assessing the effectiveness of security controls, identifying vulnerabilities, and ensuring compliance with regulatory requirements and industry standards. Security audits involve a systematic review of an organization's IT infrastructure, policies, procedures, and practices to identify potential security risks and weaknesses that could be exploited by threat actors. One key aspect of security audit planning is defining the scope and objectives of the audit, which involves determining the systems, applications, and processes to be assessed, as well as the specific goals and outcomes of the audit. Organizations can use the "nmap" command-line tool to conduct network discovery and reconnaissance, identifying active hosts, open ports, and services running on the network, and determining the scope of the audit.

Moreover, organizations need to establish audit criteria and standards based on industry best practices, regulatory requirements, and internal policies and guidelines. Audit criteria define the specific requirements and expectations against which the organization's security posture will be evaluated, while audit standards provide guidance on how audits should be conducted and documented. For example, organizations can reference frameworks such as the National Institute of Standards and Technology (NIST) Cybersecurity Framework or the International Organization for Standardization (ISO) 27001 standard to define audit criteria and standards for their security audits.

Additionally, security audit planning involves identifying and engaging stakeholders who will be involved in the audit process, including IT security personnel, system administrators, business unit representatives, and external auditors or consultants. Stakeholders play a crucial role in providing access to relevant systems and information, coordinating audit activities, and addressing findings and recommendations. Organizations can use collaboration tools such as Slack or Microsoft Teams to communicate and coordinate with stakeholders throughout the audit planning and execution process.

Furthermore, organizations need to develop an audit plan outlining the methodology, procedures, and timeline for conducting the audit. The audit plan should include details such as the audit scope and objectives, the roles and responsibilities of audit team members, the schedule of audit activities, and the criteria for evaluating security controls and practices. For example, organizations can use project management tools such as Jira or Trello to create and manage audit plans, track progress, and assign tasks to team members.

Moreover, security audit execution involves performing a series of assessment activities to evaluate the organization's security posture and identify potential vulnerabilities and weaknesses. These activities may include reviewing security policies and procedures, conducting interviews with key stakeholders, examining system configurations and access controls, and performing technical assessments such as vulnerability scanning and penetration testing. Organizations can use vulnerability scanning tools such as Nessus or Qualys to identify known security vulnerabilities and misconfigurations in their IT infrastructure, prioritize remediation efforts, and reduce the risk of exploitation by threat actors.

Additionally, organizations need to document audit findings, observations, and recommendations in a formal audit report, which provides a comprehensive overview of the audit findings and their implications for the organization's security posture. The audit report should include details such as the scope and objectives of the audit, the methodology and procedures used, a summary of findings and observations, and recommendations for improving security controls and practices. Organizations can use documentation tools such as Microsoft Word or Google Docs to create audit reports, format them according to organizational standards, and share them with key stakeholders for review and action.

Furthermore, organizations need to develop a remediation plan to address the findings and recommendations identified during the audit. The remediation plan should prioritize security vulnerabilities and weaknesses based on their severity and potential impact on the organization, allocate resources and responsibilities for remediation efforts, and establish timelines for implementing corrective actions. Organizations can use project management tools such as Asana or Monday.com to create and manage remediation plans, track progress, and monitor the status of remediation efforts.

Moreover, security audit execution involves performing a series of assessment activities to evaluate the organization's security posture and identify potential vulnerabilities and weaknesses. These activities may include reviewing security policies and procedures, conducting interviews with key stakeholders, examining system configurations and access controls, and performing technical assessments such as vulnerability scanning and penetration testing. Organizations can use vulnerability scanning tools such as Nessus or Qualys to identify known security vulnerabilities and misconfigurations in their IT infrastructure, prioritize remediation efforts, and reduce the risk of exploitation by threat actors.

Additionally, organizations need to document audit findings, observations, and recommendations in a formal audit report, which provides a comprehensive overview of the audit findings and their implications for the organization's security posture. The audit report should include details such as the scope and objectives of the audit, the methodology and procedures used, a summary of findings and observations, and recommendations for improving security controls and practices. Organizations can use documentation tools such as Microsoft Word or Google Docs to create audit reports, format them according to organizational standards, and share them with key stakeholders for review and action.

Furthermore, organizations need to develop a remediation plan to address the findings and recommendations identified during the audit. The remediation plan should prioritize security vulnerabilities and weaknesses based on their severity and potential impact on the organization, allocate resources and responsibilities for remediation efforts, and establish timelines for implementing corrective actions. Organizations can use project management tools such as Asana or Monday.com to create and manage remediation plans, track progress, and monitor the status of remediation efforts.

In summary, security audit planning and execution are essential processes for assessing and improving an organization's security posture, identifying vulnerabilities and weaknesses, and ensuring compliance with regulatory requirements and industry standards. By following a structured approach to audit planning and execution, organizations can effectively identify and mitigate security risks, enhance their overall security posture, and build trust and confidence with stakeholders and customers. Additionally, by documenting audit findings and recommendations and developing remediation plans, organizations can address security issues proactively and demonstrate their commitment to protecting sensitive data and resources from cyber threats.

Chapter 9: Introduction to Security Policies and Procedures

Security awareness training programs are essential components of organizational cybersecurity strategies, aimed at educating employees, contractors, and stakeholders about cybersecurity risks, best practices, and procedures to mitigate threats and protect sensitive information. These programs encompass a range of training activities, including classroom sessions, online courses, workshops, simulations, and awareness campaigns, designed to raise awareness and foster a culture of security within the organization. One key aspect of security awareness training is identifying the target audience and tailoring training content and delivery methods to meet their needs and preferences. Organizations can use employee surveys, risk assessments, and feedback mechanisms to gauge the level of awareness and knowledge among employees and identify areas for improvement.

Moreover, security awareness training programs should cover a variety of topics relevant to the organization's security posture, including password security, phishing awareness, social engineering tactics, data protection practices, and regulatory compliance requirements. Training content should be engaging, interactive, and easy to understand, using real-world examples, case studies, and practical exercises to reinforce key concepts and principles. Organizations can use learning management systems (LMS) or online training platforms to deliver security awareness training modules and track employee progress and completion rates.

Additionally, security awareness training programs should be regularly updated and refreshed to reflect changes in cybersecurity threats, regulations, and technology advancements. Training content should be reviewed and revised periodically to ensure its relevance and accuracy, incorporating new threats, vulnerabilities, and best practices as they emerge. Organizations can use content management systems (CMS) or version control tools to manage and update training materials efficiently, ensuring consistency and alignment with organizational objectives.

Furthermore, to maximize the effectiveness of security awareness training programs, organizations should incorporate a variety of delivery methods and formats to appeal to different learning styles and preferences. In addition to traditional classroom-based training, organizations can use e-learning platforms, webinars, video tutorials, gamified simulations, and mobile apps to deliver training content to employees anytime, anywhere. By offering flexibility and choice in training delivery, organizations can accommodate diverse learning needs and schedules and increase engagement and participation rates.

Moreover, security awareness training programs should include regular testing and assessment to measure employee knowledge retention and identify areas for improvement. Organizations can use quizzes, assessments, and simulated phishing exercises to evaluate employee understanding of key security concepts and practices and reinforce learning objectives. By tracking and analyzing training performance metrics such as quiz scores, completion rates, and click-through rates on phishing simulations, organizations can identify trends and patterns and tailor training content and delivery methods accordingly.

Furthermore, to enhance the effectiveness of security awareness training programs, organizations should promote a culture of continuous learning and reinforcement, encouraging employees to stay vigilant and proactive in identifying and reporting security threats and incidents. Training should be integrated into the onboarding process for new hires and reinforced regularly through ongoing communications, reminders, and updates. Organizations can use email newsletters, intranet portals, posters, and social media channels to reinforce key messages, share security tips, and highlight success stories.

Moreover, organizations should provide incentives and recognition for employees who demonstrate exemplary security awareness and adherence to security policies and procedures. Recognition programs, rewards, and incentives can motivate employees to actively participate in training activities, report security incidents, and contribute to a positive security culture. By acknowledging and rewarding good security behavior, organizations can reinforce desired outcomes and foster a sense of ownership and accountability for cybersecurity among employees.

Furthermore, to ensure the long-term success and sustainability of security awareness training programs, organizations should allocate adequate resources and support for program development, implementation, and evaluation. This includes securing executive sponsorship and buy-in, dedicating budget and staff resources, and establishing clear goals, objectives, and performance metrics. By investing in comprehensive security awareness training programs, organizations can empower employees to become active participants in protecting sensitive information and assets from cyber threats and contribute to a more resilient and secure organization.

In summary, security awareness training programs are essential for building a strong cybersecurity culture within organizations, equipping employees with the knowledge, skills, and awareness needed to recognize and respond to security threats effectively. By developing comprehensive training content, leveraging diverse delivery methods, and promoting a culture of continuous learning and reinforcement, organizations can enhance their overall security posture and reduce the risk of security breaches and incidents. Additionally, by fostering a sense of ownership and accountability for cybersecurity among employees and providing incentives and recognition for good security behavior, organizations can create a positive security culture that strengthens resilience and protects against evolving cyber threats.

Chapter 10: Building a Foundation for Threat Intelligence

Threat intelligence sources and collection methods are fundamental components of cybersecurity strategies, providing organizations with valuable insights into emerging threats, vulnerabilities, and malicious activities that could pose risks to their networks, systems, and data. One key aspect of threat intelligence is the identification and aggregation of relevant data from a variety of sources, including open-source intelligence (OSINT), commercial threat feeds, government agencies, industry groups, and information sharing and analysis centers (ISACs). Organizations can use a combination of manual and automated techniques to collect and aggregate threat intelligence data from multiple sources, using tools such as web scrapers, APIs, and data aggregation platforms to gather and consolidate information from diverse sources.

Moreover, open-source intelligence (OSINT) refers to publicly available information from a variety of sources, including websites, social media platforms, forums, blogs, and news articles, that can provide valuable insights into cyber threats and adversaries. Organizations can use web scraping tools such as "Scrapy" or "Beautiful Soup" to extract relevant data from websites and online forums, capturing information such as threat actor profiles, tactics, techniques, and procedures (TTPs), and indicators of compromise (IOCs).

Additionally, organizations can leverage social media monitoring tools to track discussions and mentions of relevant keywords or hashtags related to cybersecurity threats and incidents.

Additionally, commercial threat intelligence feeds are subscription-based services offered by cybersecurity vendors and research organizations, providing organizations with curated threat intelligence data and analysis tailored to their specific industry, geography, and risk profile. These feeds typically include indicators of compromise (IOCs), malware signatures, threat actor profiles, and actionable intelligence on emerging threats and vulnerabilities. Organizations can use threat intelligence platforms such as "MISP" (Malware Information Sharing Platform) or "ThreatConnect" to ingest and analyze commercial threat feeds, correlating and enriching intelligence data to identify patterns and trends and prioritize response efforts.

Furthermore, government agencies and law enforcement organizations are valuable sources of threat intelligence, providing organizations with access to classified and sensitive information on cyber threats, nation-state actors, and criminal syndicates. Government agencies such as the Federal Bureau of Investigation (FBI), Department of Homeland Security (DHS), and National Security Agency (NSA) regularly publish alerts, advisories, and reports on cybersecurity threats and incidents, sharing actionable intelligence and best practices with the private sector. Organizations can subscribe to email alerts or RSS feeds from government agencies or access threat intelligence portals such as the Cybersecurity and Infrastructure Security Agency (CISA) website to stay informed about the latest threats and vulnerabilities.

Moreover, industry groups and information sharing and analysis centers (ISACs) are collaborative forums established to facilitate the sharing of threat intelligence and best practices among organizations within specific sectors or industries. ISACs operate as trusted communities where members can share anonymized threat intelligence data, incident reports, and mitigation strategies in real-time, enabling organizations to proactively identify and respond to emerging threats and attacks. Organizations can join ISACs relevant to their industry or sector, such as the Financial Services ISAC (FS-ISAC) or the Healthcare and Public Health ISAC (H-ISAC), to access threat intelligence sharing platforms and participate in collaborative threat intelligence sharing activities.

Furthermore, threat intelligence collection methods may also include human intelligence (HUMINT) and technical intelligence (TECHINT) gathering techniques, which involve leveraging human sources, such as informants, insiders, or threat hunters, and technical tools and capabilities, such as malware analysis, network forensics, and digital forensics, to gather intelligence on cyber threats and adversaries. Organizations can deploy threat hunting teams or security analysts to conduct proactive investigations and analysis of suspicious activities, anomalies, or indicators of compromise (IOCs) within their network environments, using tools such as "Wireshark" or

"Splunk" to analyze network traffic and logs and identify potential security incidents.

Moreover, threat intelligence collection methods may also include human intelligence (HUMINT) and technical intelligence (TECHINT) gathering techniques, which involve leveraging human sources, such as informants, insiders, or threat hunters, and technical tools and capabilities, such as malware analysis, network forensics, and digital forensics, to gather intelligence on cyber threats and adversaries. Organizations can deploy threat hunting teams or security analysts to conduct proactive investigations and analysis of suspicious activities, anomalies, or indicators of compromise (IOCs) within their network environments, using tools such as "Wireshark" or "Splunk" to analyze network traffic and logs and identify potential security incidents.

Moreover, threat intelligence collection methods may also include human intelligence (HUMINT) and technical intelligence (TECHINT) gathering techniques, which involve leveraging human sources, such as informants, insiders, or threat hunters, and technical tools and capabilities, such as malware analysis, network forensics, and digital forensics, to gather intelligence on cyber threats and adversaries. Organizations can deploy threat hunting teams or security analysts to conduct proactive investigations and analysis of suspicious activities, anomalies, or indicators of compromise (IOCs) within their network environments, using tools such as "Wireshark" or "Splunk" to analyze network traffic and logs and identify potential security incidents.

In summary, threat intelligence sources and collection methods play a crucial role in helping organizations identify, analyze, and respond to cyber threats effectively. By leveraging a combination of open-source intelligence (OSINT), commercial threat feeds, government alerts, industry collaboration, and internal investigations, organizations can gather actionable intelligence on emerging threats, vulnerabilities, and malicious activities and take proactive measures to mitigate risks and protect their assets. Additionally, by investing in advanced threat intelligence platforms, tools, and capabilities, organizations can enhance their ability to collect, analyze, and operationalize threat intelligence data, enabling faster detection and response to cyber threats and improving overall cybersecurity posture.

Threat intelligence analysis and integration are critical processes within cybersecurity operations, enabling organizations to transform raw intelligence data into actionable insights and integrate them into their security infrastructure to improve threat detection and response capabilities. One key aspect of threat intelligence analysis is the evaluation and validation of intelligence data to assess its relevance, credibility, and potential impact on the organization. Security analysts use a variety of analytical techniques and tools to analyze intelligence data, including statistical analysis, pattern recognition, data visualization, and machine learning algorithms, to identify trends, correlations, and anomalies that may indicate emerging threats or attack patterns.

Moreover, threat intelligence analysis involves enriching and contextualizing intelligence data by correlating it with internal security telemetry, such as network traffic logs, endpoint logs, and security event data, to provide a more comprehensive understanding of the threat landscape. Analysts can use SIEM (Security Information and Event Management) platforms such as "Splunk" or "Elasticsearch" to ingest, correlate, and analyze intelligence data alongside internal security logs and alerts, enabling them to identify and prioritize security incidents and respond more effectively to threats. Additionally, analysts can use threat intelligence platforms (TIPs) such as "Anomali" or "ThreatConnect" to aggregate, enrich, and manage intelligence data from multiple sources, automate analysis workflows, and disseminate actionable intelligence to relevant stakeholders.

Additionally, threat intelligence analysis involves categorizing and prioritizing intelligence data based on its severity, relevance, and potential impact on the organization's assets, operations, and reputation. Analysts use risk assessment frameworks such as the Common Vulnerability Scoring System (CVSS) or the Cyber Kill Chain model to evaluate the likelihood and impact of threats and vulnerabilities and prioritize response actions accordingly. By assigning risk scores or ratings to intelligence data, analysts can prioritize remediation efforts, allocate resources more effectively, and focus on addressing the most critical and imminent threats to the organization.

Furthermore, threat intelligence integration involves operationalizing intelligence data by incorporating it into existing security controls, processes, and workflows to improve threat detection, prevention, and response capabilities. Organizations can use threat intelligence feeds, indicators of compromise (IOCs), and signatures to enhance their security controls, such as firewalls, intrusion detection systems (IDS), and endpoint protection platforms (EPP), by blocking known malicious IP addresses, domains, or file hashes. For example, security administrators can use firewall rules or IPS (Intrusion Prevention System) signatures to block incoming traffic from known malicious IP addresses or domains identified in threat intelligence feeds, preventing potential attacks from reaching the organization's network.

Moreover, threat intelligence integration involves leveraging intelligence data to inform security monitoring and incident response activities, enabling organizations to detect and respond to security incidents more quickly and effectively. Security operations teams can use threat intelligence feeds and indicators of compromise (IOCs) to create custom detection rules and alerts in their SIEM or security analytics platforms, allowing them to identify and investigate suspicious activities or anomalies that may indicate potential security breaches. Additionally, organizations can use threat intelligence to enrich security incident data with additional context, such as the tactics, techniques, and procedures (TTPs) used by threat actors, enabling security analysts to prioritize and respond to incidents more efficiently.

Furthermore, threat intelligence integration involves integrating intelligence data into security incident response processes and playbooks to guide and streamline response actions during security incidents. Organizations can create incident response playbooks or runbooks that incorporate intelligence-driven response actions and decision criteria, allowing security teams to quickly assess the severity and impact of incidents, determine appropriate response actions, and coordinate response efforts more effectively. For example, incident response playbooks may include predefined steps for blocking malicious IP addresses, isolating compromised systems, and conducting forensic analysis based on intelligence data and threat intelligence indicators.

Additionally, threat intelligence integration involves sharing intelligence data and insights with external partners, such as industry peers, government agencies, and information sharing and analysis centers (ISACs), to enhance collective defense and improve situational awareness. Organizations can participate in threat intelligence sharing programs and platforms, such as the Cyber Threat Alliance (CTA) or Information Sharing and Analysis Organizations (ISAOs), to exchange intelligence data, collaborate on threat research, and coordinate response efforts with other organizations facing similar threats. By sharing intelligence data and collaborating with external partners, organizations can leverage collective expertise and resources to identify and mitigate threats more effectively and strengthen the overall cybersecurity ecosystem.

Moreover, threat intelligence integration involves continuous monitoring and refinement of intelligence data and processes to adapt to evolving threats and security challenges. Organizations should regularly review and update their threat intelligence feeds, indicators, and detection rules to incorporate new threat intelligence sources, emerging threats, and changing attack techniques and tactics. Additionally, organizations should conduct post-incident reviews and analysis to evaluate the effectiveness of threat intelligence in detecting and responding to security incidents and identify areas for improvement in threat intelligence analysis and integration processes.

In summary, threat intelligence analysis and integration are essential capabilities for organizations seeking to enhance their cybersecurity posture and protect against advanced threats and cyber attacks. By analyzing and integrating intelligence data into existing security controls, processes, and workflows, organizations can improve threat detection, prevention, and response capabilities, reduce the risk of security breaches, and mitigate the impact of cyber threats on their operations and assets. Additionally, by collaborating with external partners and sharing intelligence data, organizations can enhance collective defense and contribute to a more resilient and secure cybersecurity ecosystem.

BOOK 2
MASTERING THREAT IDENTIFICATION STRATEGIES AND TECHNIQUES FOR SY0-701

ROB BOTWRIGHT

Chapter 1: Understanding Threat Landscape

Cybersecurity threats pose significant risks to organizations and individuals worldwide, encompassing a wide range of malicious activities and tactics aimed at exploiting vulnerabilities in technology, systems, and networks to steal data, disrupt operations, and cause financial or reputational harm. One prominent cybersecurity threat is malware, which includes various types of malicious software designed to infiltrate, damage, or gain unauthorized access to computer systems and networks. Examples of malware include viruses, worms, Trojans, ransomware, and spyware, which can infect devices and compromise sensitive information, disrupt critical services, and extort victims for financial gain. To mitigate the risk of malware infections, organizations deploy antivirus software, firewalls, and intrusion detection systems to detect and block malicious code and behavior.

Another prevalent cybersecurity threat is phishing, a social engineering technique used by cybercriminals to deceive individuals into disclosing sensitive information, such as usernames, passwords, or financial data, or downloading malware-infected attachments or links. Phishing attacks often involve email or text messages impersonating legitimate entities, such as banks, government agencies, or trusted brands, and urging recipients to take immediate action, such as clicking on a link to verify their account or updating their credentials. To defend against phishing attacks, organizations conduct security awareness training for employees, implement email filtering and authentication measures, and use web browsers with built-in phishing protection features.

Furthermore, ransomware attacks have emerged as a significant cybersecurity threat, targeting organizations of all sizes and industries by encrypting their data and demanding ransom payments in exchange for decryption keys. Ransomware typically spreads through malicious email attachments, exploit kits, or compromised websites and can cause severe disruptions to business operations, data loss, and financial losses. To protect against ransomware attacks, organizations implement data backup and recovery strategies, deploy endpoint security solutions with ransomware detection capabilities, and conduct regular security assessments to identify and patch vulnerabilities in their systems and networks.

Additionally, distributed denial-of-service (DDoS) attacks pose a persistent threat to organizations' online presence and infrastructure by flooding their networks, servers, or applications with a massive volume of malicious traffic, causing service disruptions or downtime. DDoS attacks can be launched using botnets, compromised devices, or amplification techniques to overwhelm targeted systems and exhaust their resources, rendering them inaccessible to legitimate users. To defend against DDoS attacks, organizations deploy DDoS mitigation solutions, such as scrubbing centers, content delivery networks (CDNs), or cloud-based DDoS protection services, to filter and block malicious traffic before it reaches their networks.

Moreover, insider threats represent a significant cybersecurity risk for organizations, involving employees, contractors, or business partners who misuse their access privileges or insider knowledge to steal data, sabotage systems, or compromise security controls. Insider threats can result from malicious intent, such as disgruntled employees seeking revenge or financial gain, or unintentional actions, such as negligent employees falling victim to phishing scams or inadvertently leaking sensitive information. To mitigate insider threats, organizations implement access controls, monitoring tools, and user behavior analytics to detect and respond to suspicious activities or anomalies indicative of insider misuse or abuse.

Furthermore, supply chain attacks have emerged as a growing cybersecurity concern, targeting organizations through vulnerabilities in their third-party vendors, suppliers, or service providers. Supply chain attacks involve attackers compromising trusted vendors' systems or software supply chains to infiltrate targeted organizations' networks and steal data or deploy malware. These attacks can have far-reaching consequences, impacting multiple organizations across the supply chain and compromising the integrity and security of products, services, or data. To mitigate supply chain attacks, organizations conduct risk assessments of their third-party vendors, implement supply chain security controls, and establish incident response plans to respond to potential breaches or compromises.

Additionally, zero-day exploits pose a significant cybersecurity threat by targeting previously unknown vulnerabilities in software, hardware, or firmware that have not been patched or mitigated by vendors. Zero-day exploits allow attackers to exploit vulnerabilities to gain unauthorized access to systems, steal sensitive information, or launch malicious activities without detection or defense measures in place. To defend against zero-day exploits, organizations deploy vulnerability management solutions, patch management processes, and intrusion detection systems to identify and remediate vulnerabilities before they are exploited by attackers.

Moreover, advanced persistent threats (APTs) represent sophisticated and stealthy cyber attacks orchestrated by nation-state actors, cybercriminal groups, or well-funded adversaries with the goal of infiltrating targeted organizations' networks and stealing sensitive information or intellectual property. APTs typically involve multiple stages, including reconnaissance, initial access, lateral movement, and data exfiltration, and may employ advanced techniques, such as zero-day exploits, social engineering, and custom malware, to evade detection and maintain persistence. To defend against APTs, organizations implement defense-in-depth strategies, network segmentation, endpoint detection and response (EDR) solutions, and threat hunting capabilities to detect and respond to APT activities in their networks.

In summary, cybersecurity threats continue to evolve in sophistication, scale, and impact, posing significant challenges for organizations and individuals alike. By understanding the nature of cybersecurity threats and implementing proactive security measures, organizations can enhance their resilience and readiness to defend against cyber attacks and protect their assets, data, and reputation. Additionally, collaboration, information sharing, and continuous learning are essential for staying ahead of emerging threats and adapting to the evolving cybersecurity landscape.

The evolving threat landscape presents a dynamic and multifaceted challenge for organizations and cybersecurity professionals, requiring continuous analysis, adaptation, and response to emerging threats and attack vectors. One key aspect of analyzing the evolving threat landscape is monitoring and tracking new and emerging cyber threats, vulnerabilities, and attack techniques that could pose risks to organizations' systems, networks, and data. Security analysts use a variety of threat intelligence sources and tools to gather, analyze, and disseminate information about evolving threats, including open-source intelligence (OSINT), commercial threat feeds, government advisories, and industry reports. By staying informed about the latest threat intelligence, organizations can better understand the tactics, techniques, and procedures (TTPs) used by threat actors and proactively mitigate potential risks.

Moreover, threat actors are constantly evolving their tactics and techniques to bypass traditional security controls and exploit vulnerabilities in target systems, making it essential for organizations to adapt their defensive strategies accordingly. Security professionals use threat modeling techniques, such as STRIDE (Spoofing, Tampering, Repudiation, Information Disclosure, Denial of Service, Elevation of Privilege), to assess and prioritize potential threats and vulnerabilities based on their likelihood and impact on organizational assets. By conducting threat modeling exercises, organizations can identify gaps in their defenses, prioritize security investments, and develop risk mitigation strategies to address evolving threats effectively.

Additionally, threat intelligence sharing and collaboration play a crucial role in analyzing and responding to the evolving threat landscape, enabling organizations to leverage collective expertise, resources, and insights to detect, prevent, and respond to cyber threats more effectively. Information sharing and analysis centers (ISACs), industry forums, and threat intelligence sharing platforms facilitate the exchange of threat intelligence data, incident reports, and best practices among organizations within specific sectors or industries. By participating in threat intelligence sharing initiatives, organizations can gain valuable insights into emerging threats, indicators of compromise (IOCs), and attack trends, enabling them to strengthen their defenses and better protect against cyber attacks.

Furthermore, security analytics and machine learning technologies are increasingly being used to analyze large volumes of security data and identify patterns, anomalies, and indicators of compromise (IOCs) indicative of malicious activity. Security information and event management (SIEM) platforms, such as Splunk or ELK Stack, aggregate and correlate security logs, alerts, and events from various sources to provide visibility into potential security incidents and threats. By applying machine learning algorithms and statistical analysis techniques to security data, organizations can detect and respond to suspicious activities in real-time, reducing the time to detect and mitigate threats and minimizing the impact of cyber attacks.

Moreover, proactive threat hunting techniques are employed to identify and disrupt advanced threats and adversaries lurking within organizations' networks. Threat hunting involves proactively searching for signs of malicious activity or compromise by analyzing network traffic, endpoint logs, and other telemetry data for indicators of compromise (IOCs) and anomalous behavior. Security analysts use a combination of manual investigation techniques and automated tools, such as EDR (Endpoint Detection and Response) solutions or network traffic analysis tools, to hunt for signs of compromise, identify stealthy threats, and mitigate security risks before they escalate into full-blown incidents.

Additionally, organizations must continually assess and improve their cybersecurity posture to adapt to the evolving threat landscape and address new and emerging risks effectively. Regular security assessments, penetration testing, and vulnerability scanning help identify weaknesses and gaps in organizations' defenses, allowing them to prioritize remediation efforts and strengthen their security controls. By conducting tabletop exercises and incident response drills, organizations can test their incident response plans, assess their readiness to respond to cyber threats, and identify areas for improvement in their security posture and incident response capabilities.

Furthermore, regulatory compliance requirements and industry standards play a critical role in shaping organizations' cybersecurity strategies and practices, providing guidelines and frameworks for managing cybersecurity risks and protecting sensitive information. Compliance frameworks such as the NIST Cybersecurity Framework, ISO/IEC 27001, and GDPR (General Data Protection Regulation) outline best practices and controls for managing cybersecurity risks, ensuring the confidentiality, integrity, and availability of data, and demonstrating compliance with regulatory requirements. By aligning with industry standards and compliance frameworks, organizations can establish a baseline for their security practices, identify areas for improvement, and demonstrate their commitment to cybersecurity best practices and risk management.

Moreover, cybersecurity awareness and training programs are essential for educating employees about the evolving threat landscape, common attack techniques, and best practices for protecting against cyber threats. Security awareness training helps employees recognize phishing attempts, social engineering tactics, and other cybersecurity risks, empowering them to make informed decisions and take proactive steps to safeguard sensitive information and assets. By fostering a culture of security awareness and accountability, organizations can strengthen their human firewall and reduce the risk of insider threats, inadvertent data breaches, and security incidents caused by human error.

In summary, analyzing the evolving threat landscape requires a multifaceted approach that combines threat intelligence, security analytics, threat hunting, compliance, and employee training to effectively detect, prevent, and respond to cyber threats. By staying vigilant, proactive, and adaptable, organizations can mitigate the risks posed by the evolving threat landscape and enhance their resilience to cyber attacks. Additionally, collaboration, information sharing, and continuous learning are essential for staying ahead of emerging threats and evolving cybersecurity challenges in today's rapidly changing threat landscape.

Chapter 2: Types of Cyber Threats

Common cyber attack vectors encompass a diverse range of techniques and strategies employed by threat actors to compromise systems, steal data, or disrupt operations, posing significant risks to organizations and individuals alike. One prevalent attack vector is phishing, a social engineering technique used to deceive users into disclosing sensitive information or downloading malware by impersonating trusted entities or individuals through email, text messages, or malicious websites. To mitigate the risk of phishing attacks, organizations deploy email filtering solutions, conduct security awareness training for employees, and implement multi-factor authentication (MFA) to verify user identities and protect against unauthorized access. Additionally, malware represents another common attack vector, encompassing various types of malicious software designed to infiltrate systems, compromise data, or disrupt operations, including viruses, worms, Trojans, ransomware, and spyware. Organizations use antivirus software, firewalls, and endpoint detection and response (EDR) solutions to detect and block malware infections, conduct regular system scans, and update software patches to protect against known vulnerabilities exploited by malware.

Furthermore, ransomware attacks have emerged as a significant cyber threat, targeting organizations of all sizes and industries by encrypting their data and demanding ransom payments in exchange for decryption keys. Ransomware typically spreads through phishing emails, exploit kits, or remote desktop protocol (RDP) vulnerabilities, encrypting files and demanding payment in cryptocurrency to restore access. To defend against ransomware attacks, organizations implement data backup and recovery solutions, deploy endpoint security controls, and conduct user training to recognize and report suspicious emails or links. Moreover, distributed denial-of-service (DDoS) attacks represent a common vector for disrupting online services and networks by flooding them with a high volume of malicious traffic, causing service degradation or downtime. Organizations use DDoS mitigation services, web application firewalls (WAFs), and network traffic monitoring tools to detect and mitigate DDoS attacks, filter malicious traffic, and maintain service availability.

Additionally, credential theft and brute force attacks are common attack vectors used by threat actors to gain unauthorized access to systems, networks, or accounts by exploiting weak or stolen credentials. Attackers use automated tools to guess passwords or credentials through trial and error, exploiting weak password policies or using stolen credentials obtained through phishing, data breaches, or credential stuffing attacks. Organizations deploy strong password policies, multi-factor authentication (MFA), and account lockout mechanisms to prevent unauthorized access and protect against credential-based attacks. Furthermore, supply chain attacks have become increasingly prevalent, targeting third-party vendors, suppliers, or service providers to infiltrate organizations' networks and compromise their systems or data. Supply chain attacks involve attackers compromising trusted vendors' systems or software supply chains to distribute malware, steal sensitive information, or conduct espionage activities. Organizations conduct risk assessments of their supply chain partners, implement security controls, and establish vendor management processes to mitigate the risk of supply chain attacks and ensure the integrity of their supply chain.

Moreover, insider threats pose a significant risk to organizations, involving employees, contractors, or business partners who misuse their access privileges or insider knowledge to steal data, sabotage systems, or compromise security controls. Insider threats can result from malicious intent, such as disgruntled employees seeking revenge or financial gain, or unintentional actions, such as negligent employees falling victim to phishing scams or inadvertently leaking sensitive information. Organizations implement access controls, user monitoring tools, and security awareness training to detect and respond to insider threats, monitor user activity, and enforce least privilege access policies to limit the potential impact of insider attacks. Additionally, zero-day exploits represent a critical attack vector used by threat actors to exploit previously unknown vulnerabilities in software, hardware, or firmware before vendors release patches or mitigations. Zero-day exploits allow attackers to gain unauthorized access to systems, steal data, or launch malicious activities without detection or defense measures in place. Organizations deploy vulnerability management solutions, conduct regular security assessments, and monitor threat intelligence feeds to identify and remediate zero-day vulnerabilities before they are exploited by attackers.

Furthermore, advanced persistent threats (APTs) represent sophisticated and stealthy cyber attacks orchestrated by nation-state actors, cybercriminal groups, or well-funded adversaries with the goal of infiltrating targeted organizations' networks and stealing sensitive information or intellectual property. APTs involve multiple stages, including reconnaissance, initial access, lateral movement, and data exfiltration, and may employ advanced techniques, such as zero-day exploits, social engineering, and custom malware, to evade detection and maintain persistence. To defend against APTs, organizations implement defense-in-depth strategies, network segmentation, endpoint detection and response (EDR) solutions, and threat hunting capabilities to detect and respond to APT activities in their networks. In summary, understanding common cyber attack vectors and implementing appropriate security measures are essential for organizations to protect against cyber threats, safeguard their data and assets, and maintain business continuity in today's evolving threat landscape.

Emerging threat trends encompass evolving tactics, techniques, and procedures (TTPs) used by cybercriminals, threat actors, and adversaries to exploit vulnerabilities, evade detection, and achieve their malicious objectives in the ever-changing cybersecurity landscape. One emerging threat trend is the proliferation of ransomware-as-a-service (RaaS) models, which enable cybercriminals to access ransomware tools and infrastructure through underground forums or dark web marketplaces, allowing them to launch ransomware attacks with minimal technical expertise or resources. RaaS platforms provide affiliates with pre-configured ransomware variants, distribution channels, and payment processing capabilities, enabling them to execute ransomware campaigns and monetize their attacks by extorting victims for ransom payments in cryptocurrency. To mitigate the risk of ransomware attacks, organizations should implement a multi-layered defense strategy, including robust backup and recovery solutions, endpoint security controls, and employee training to recognize and respond to phishing attempts or suspicious activity.

Furthermore, supply chain attacks have become a growing concern for organizations, involving threat actors targeting third-party vendors, suppliers, or service providers to infiltrate their networks and compromise their systems or data. Supply chain attacks exploit vulnerabilities in the software or hardware supply chain to distribute malware, steal sensitive information, or conduct espionage activities, posing significant risks to organizations' security and resilience. To mitigate the risk of supply chain attacks, organizations should conduct thorough risk assessments of their supply chain partners, implement security controls and monitoring mechanisms, and establish vendor management processes to ensure the integrity and security of their supply chain.

Additionally, the rise of sophisticated phishing attacks, such as business email compromise (BEC) and spear phishing, has contributed to the increase in successful cyber intrusions and data breaches targeting organizations of all sizes and industries. BEC attacks involve impersonating legitimate entities or individuals, such as executives or vendors, to deceive employees into transferring funds, disclosing sensitive information, or initiating wire transfers, resulting in financial losses and reputational damage for organizations. Spear phishing attacks target specific individuals or groups within an organization, leveraging social engineering techniques and personalized messages to trick recipients into revealing credentials, downloading malware, or taking other malicious actions. To defend against phishing attacks, organizations should deploy email filtering and authentication solutions, conduct security awareness training for employees, and implement multi-factor authentication (MFA) to verify user identities and protect against unauthorized access.

Moreover, the increasing adoption of cloud computing services and technologies has introduced new security challenges and risks for organizations, including data breaches, misconfigurations, and unauthorized access to cloud resources. Cloud security misconfigurations, such as improperly configured storage buckets or access controls, can expose sensitive data to unauthorized users or external threats, leading to data leaks or breaches. To mitigate the risk of cloud security misconfigurations, organizations should implement robust cloud security controls, such as encryption, access management, and logging and monitoring, to protect their data and assets in the cloud environment. Additionally, the use of cloud-native security solutions, such as cloud access security brokers (CASBs) and cloud workload protection platforms (CWPPs), can help organizations enforce security policies, detect and respond to cloud security incidents, and ensure compliance with regulatory requirements.

Furthermore, the convergence of operational technology (OT) and information technology (IT) systems has introduced new attack surfaces and vulnerabilities for critical infrastructure sectors, including energy, utilities, manufacturing, and transportation. Cyber attacks targeting OT systems, such as industrial control systems (ICS) and supervisory control and data acquisition (SCADA) systems, can disrupt essential services, cause physical damage, and pose significant risks to public safety and national security. To enhance the security and resilience of OT environments, organizations should implement robust OT cybersecurity measures, such as network segmentation, access controls, intrusion detection systems (IDS), and anomaly detection technologies, to detect and mitigate cyber threats targeting OT assets and infrastructure.

Additionally, the emergence of novel attack techniques, such as fileless malware, living-off-the-land attacks, and supply chain compromises, presents new challenges for organizations' cybersecurity defenses and incident response capabilities. Fileless malware leverages legitimate system tools and processes to execute malicious code in memory, making it difficult to detect and remediate using traditional antivirus or endpoint security solutions. Living-off-the-land attacks involve leveraging built-in system utilities and legitimate applications to conduct malicious activities, such as lateral movement, privilege escalation, and data exfiltration, without triggering traditional security controls or antivirus signatures. Supply chain compromises target trusted software vendors or suppliers to distribute malware, backdoors, or supply chain implants to unsuspecting organizations, compromising their systems and networks. To defend against these emerging threats, organizations should implement advanced threat detection and response capabilities, such as endpoint detection and response (EDR), network traffic analysis, and threat hunting, to detect and respond to sophisticated attacks in real-time.

In summary, understanding and mitigating emerging threat trends require organizations to adopt a proactive and adaptive approach to cybersecurity, leveraging threat intelligence, security best practices, and advanced technologies to detect, prevent, and respond to evolving cyber threats effectively. By staying informed about emerging threats, implementing robust security controls, and fostering a culture of cybersecurity awareness and resilience, organizations can enhance their ability to withstand cyber attacks and protect their data, assets, and reputation in today's dynamic and complex threat landscape.

Chapter 3: Anatomy of Malware

Malware classification and characteristics play a pivotal role in understanding the diverse landscape of malicious software and the techniques employed by cybercriminals to compromise systems, steal data, or disrupt operations. One fundamental aspect of malware classification is distinguishing between different types of malware based on their behavior, functionality, and propagation methods. For instance, viruses are self-replicating programs that attach themselves to executable files or documents, allowing them to spread from one system to another when infected files are shared or executed. To identify and mitigate virus infections, antivirus software can be deployed to scan files and detect known virus signatures, while also utilizing behavioral analysis to identify suspicious activities indicative of virus behavior.

Furthermore, worms represent another category of malware that propagate independently across networks and systems, exploiting vulnerabilities in software or network protocols to infect vulnerable hosts and spread malicious payloads. Worms can rapidly spread and proliferate within networks, causing widespread disruption and damage by exploiting unpatched vulnerabilities or weak security controls. Organizations can mitigate the risk of worm infections by applying security patches and updates promptly, implementing network segmentation, and deploying intrusion detection and prevention systems (IDPS) to detect and block worm activity at the network perimeter.

Additionally, Trojans, named after the mythological wooden horse used to infiltrate the city of Troy, are malicious programs disguised as legitimate software or files, often distributed via email attachments, file-sharing networks, or malicious websites. Trojans typically perform unauthorized activities, such as stealing sensitive information, compromising system security, or facilitating remote access by creating backdoors for attackers. To defend against Trojan infections, organizations should deploy endpoint security solutions, conduct user training to recognize and avoid malicious emails or attachments, and implement application whitelisting to control the execution of trusted software.

Moreover, ransomware has emerged as a pervasive and destructive form of malware, encrypting victims' files or systems and demanding ransom payments in exchange for decryption keys. Ransomware attacks often involve sophisticated encryption algorithms and techniques to render victims' data inaccessible, resulting in financial losses, reputational damage, and operational disruptions. Organizations can protect against ransomware attacks by implementing data backup and recovery solutions, deploying endpoint security controls, and conducting regular security awareness training for employees to recognize and respond to ransomware threats effectively.

Furthermore, spyware represents a type of malware designed to monitor and gather sensitive information from infected systems without users' knowledge or consent, including keystrokes, browsing history, and login credentials. Spyware infections can compromise users' privacy, expose sensitive data to unauthorized access, and facilitate identity theft or fraud. To detect and remove spyware infections, organizations should deploy anti-spyware tools, conduct regular system scans, and educate users about safe browsing habits and the risks of downloading untrusted software or files.

Additionally, adware and potentially unwanted programs (PUPs) are forms of malware that display intrusive advertisements, collect user data, or modify browser settings without users' consent, resulting in a degraded user experience and increased exposure to security risks. Adware and PUPs often accompany freeware or shareware downloads, bundling additional software components or browser extensions that generate revenue through advertising or data collection. To prevent adware and PUP infections, organizations should exercise caution when downloading software from untrusted sources, carefully review end-user license agreements (EULAs), and use ad-blocking or anti-malware tools to block unwanted advertisements and prevent unwanted software installations.

Moreover, rootkits represent a particularly stealthy and sophisticated form of malware designed to conceal their presence and evade detection by security software and system administrators. Rootkits typically manipulate operating system components or system firmware to gain privileged access and control over infected systems, allowing attackers to maintain persistent access and conceal their malicious activities from security controls and monitoring tools. To detect and remove rootkits, organizations should use rootkit detection tools and forensic analysis techniques to identify suspicious system behavior, abnormal network traffic, or unauthorized modifications to system files or configurations.

In summary, understanding the classification and characteristics of malware is essential for developing effective cybersecurity strategies and defenses against evolving threats. By recognizing the behavior, propagation methods, and impact of different types of malware, organizations can implement appropriate security measures, such as antivirus software, intrusion detection systems, and user training, to detect, prevent, and respond to malware infections effectively. Additionally, maintaining up-to-date security patches, conducting regular system scans, and practicing safe computing habits are crucial for mitigating the risk of malware infections and safeguarding against potential security breaches and data compromises.

Malware analysis techniques are essential for understanding the behavior, functionality, and impact of malicious software on systems and networks, enabling cybersecurity professionals to develop effective detection, prevention, and mitigation strategies against cyber threats. One fundamental malware analysis technique is static analysis, which involves examining the code and structure of malware samples without executing them, allowing analysts to identify suspicious or malicious characteristics, such as obfuscated code, suspicious API calls, or hardcoded URLs. Static analysis tools, such as disassemblers, decompilers, and hex editors, can be used to inspect malware samples' binary code, file headers, and resource sections, providing insights into their functionality and potential indicators of compromise (IOCs). For example, analysts can use the objdump command in Linux to disassemble executable files and inspect their assembly code for malicious instructions or behaviors.

Furthermore, dynamic analysis is another crucial technique for analyzing malware behavior in a controlled environment, such as a virtual machine or sandbox, allowing analysts to observe and monitor the malware's execution and interactions with the system in real-time. Dynamic analysis techniques involve executing malware samples in a controlled environment and monitoring their behavior, such as file system modifications, network communications, process creation, and registry changes, to understand their capabilities and objectives. Sandboxing tools, such as Cuckoo Sandbox or VMRay Analyzer, can automate the dynamic analysis process by executing malware samples in isolated environments and capturing their behavior through system logs, network traffic captures, and memory dumps. Analysts can then analyze the collected data to identify malicious activities, communication patterns, and IOCs associated with the malware sample.

Additionally, behavioral analysis focuses on observing and analyzing the behavior of malware samples within their execution environment to identify anomalous or malicious activities indicative of a security threat. Behavioral analysis techniques involve monitoring system events, API calls, registry modifications, and network traffic generated by malware samples to understand their intended purpose, propagation methods, and impact on infected systems. Analysts can use behavioral analysis tools, such as Process Monitor, Wireshark, or Sysinternals Suite, to capture and analyze malware behavior in real-time, allowing them to identify and mitigate potential security risks posed by malicious software. For example, analysts can use the procmon command in Windows to monitor system events and registry modifications caused by malware processes, enabling them to identify malicious activities and IOCs.

Moreover, code analysis involves examining the source code or assembly code of malware samples to identify vulnerabilities, exploits, or logic flaws that could be exploited by attackers to compromise systems or evade detection. Code analysis techniques include manual code review, static analysis, and reverse engineering, allowing analysts to identify security weaknesses, backdoors, or hidden functionalities within malware samples. Reverse engineering tools, such as IDA Pro, Ghidra, or Radare2, can be used to disassemble, decompile, and analyze malware binaries, providing insights into their inner workings and potential attack vectors. Analysts can use code analysis techniques to identify and patch vulnerabilities in software applications, firmware, or operating systems exploited by malware samples, helping to prevent future infections and improve overall system security.

Furthermore, memory analysis is another critical technique for analyzing malware behavior and identifying malicious activities that occur in volatile memory, such as RAM, registry keys, or process memory, which are not persisted on disk. Memory analysis techniques involve capturing and analyzing memory dumps or process memory snapshots to identify malware artifacts, such as injected code, process hooks, or malicious DLLs, that may be indicative of a security compromise. Memory forensics tools, such as Volatility Framework or Rekall, can be used to analyze memory dumps and extract relevant information, such as running processes, network connections, or injected code, associated with malware samples. Analysts can use memory analysis techniques to identify and remediate memory-resident malware infections, rootkits, or stealthy persistence mechanisms that evade traditional antivirus or endpoint security controls.

Additionally, network analysis involves monitoring and analyzing network traffic generated by malware samples to identify communication patterns, command and control (C2) servers, or malicious domains associated with cyber attacks. Network analysis techniques include packet capture, traffic analysis, and protocol decoding, allowing analysts to identify malicious activities, such as data exfiltration, command execution, or lateral movement, occurring over the network. Network forensics tools, such as Wireshark, tcpdump, or Suricata, can be used to capture and analyze network traffic in real-time, enabling analysts to identify malicious payloads, exploit attempts, or reconnaissance activities conducted by malware samples. Analysts can use network analysis techniques to detect and block malicious network traffic, identify compromised systems, and disrupt cyber attacks before they cause significant damage or loss.

In summary, malware analysis techniques are essential for understanding and mitigating the threats posed by malicious software, enabling cybersecurity professionals to identify, analyze, and respond to cyber attacks effectively. By leveraging static analysis, dynamic analysis, behavioral analysis, code analysis, memory analysis, and network analysis techniques, analysts can gain insights into malware behavior, capabilities, and objectives, helping to enhance cybersecurity defenses, protect critical assets, and mitigate the risks associated with cyber threats.

Chapter 4: Identifying Social Engineering Tactics

Psychological principles play a significant role in social engineering, a tactic used by cyber attackers to manipulate individuals into divulging confidential information, compromising security protocols, or performing actions that may lead to a security breach. One psychological principle commonly exploited in social engineering attacks is authority, where attackers impersonate figures of authority, such as IT administrators, company executives, or law enforcement officers, to coerce victims into complying with their demands. For instance, attackers may use pretexting techniques to impersonate IT support personnel and request sensitive information or credentials from unsuspecting employees under the guise of troubleshooting or system maintenance. To mitigate the risk of authority-based social engineering attacks, organizations should implement strict access controls, user authentication mechanisms, and employee training programs to educate staff about the importance of verifying the identity and authority of individuals requesting sensitive information or access privileges.

Furthermore, social proof is another psychological principle leveraged by attackers to influence individuals' behavior and decision-making processes by creating the perception of social validation or consensus. Social proof exploits the tendency of individuals to conform to the actions or beliefs of others in social situations, making them more susceptible to persuasion or manipulation by perceived authority figures or peer pressure. For example, attackers may use phishing emails with fake testimonials or fabricated endorsements from trusted sources to deceive recipients into believing the legitimacy of the message and taking the desired action, such as clicking on malicious links or disclosing personal information. To counter social proof-based social engineering tactics, organizations should educate employees about common phishing techniques, encourage skepticism towards unsolicited messages or requests, and implement email filtering and spam detection solutions to identify and block malicious content.

Additionally, reciprocity is a psychological principle that involves the obligation to reciprocate favors, gifts, or concessions, often exploited by attackers to induce compliance or gain trust from potential victims. Reciprocity-based social engineering tactics involve offering incentives, rewards, or false promises to manipulate individuals into disclosing sensitive information, granting access privileges, or performing actions that benefit the attacker. For instance, attackers may use pretexting techniques to impersonate colleagues or business partners and request favors or assistance from employees, exploiting their sense of reciprocity and obligation to reciprocate past favors or goodwill gestures. To mitigate the risk of reciprocity-based social engineering attacks, organizations should establish clear policies and procedures for handling requests for information or assistance, conduct regular employee training on social engineering awareness, and implement controls to verify the legitimacy of requests before granting access or divulging sensitive information.

Moreover, scarcity is a psychological principle that involves creating the perception of limited availability or urgency to influence individuals' decision-making processes and behavior. Scarcity-based social engineering tactics exploit individuals' fear of missing out or desire to obtain scarce resources or opportunities, making them more susceptible to persuasion or manipulation by attackers offering exclusive deals, limited-time offers, or urgent requests for action. For example, attackers may use phishing emails with urgent deadlines or limited-time offers to create a sense of urgency and compel recipients to click on malicious links or disclose sensitive information to avoid missing out on purported benefits or opportunities. To counter scarcity-based social engineering tactics, organizations should educate employees about common manipulation techniques used by attackers, encourage critical thinking and skepticism towards unsolicited messages or offers, and implement security controls to detect and block malicious content or phishing attempts.

Additionally, familiarity is a psychological principle that involves individuals' tendency to trust and feel comfortable with people, brands, or situations they are familiar with, making them more susceptible to manipulation by attackers who exploit this sense of trust and familiarity to deceive or manipulate victims. Familiarity-based social engineering tactics involve impersonating trusted entities, such as colleagues, vendors, or service providers, to establish rapport and gain the victim's trust before exploiting their vulnerabilities or eliciting sensitive information. For instance, attackers may use pretexting techniques to impersonate familiar contacts or organizations and request information or assistance from employees, exploiting their sense of trust and familiarity to lower their guard and increase the likelihood of compliance. To mitigate the risk of familiarity-based social engineering attacks, organizations should implement controls to verify the authenticity of communications or requests from external sources, conduct regular security awareness training for employees, and encourage skepticism towards unsolicited messages or requests for information.

Furthermore, urgency is a psychological principle that involves creating a sense of pressure or immediacy to compel individuals to act quickly or impulsively, often exploited by attackers to manipulate victims into making hasty decisions or disclosing sensitive information without due diligence or verification. Urgency-based social engineering tactics involve creating artificial deadlines, emergency situations, or threats of consequences to induce fear or anxiety in victims and coerce them into complying with the attacker's demands. For example, attackers may use phishing emails with urgent warnings or threats of account suspension, data loss, or legal action to create a sense of urgency and pressure recipients into clicking on malicious links or providing login credentials to purportedly resolve the issue. To counter urgency-based social engineering tactics, organizations should educate employees about common manipulation techniques used by attackers, encourage them to verify the authenticity of urgent requests or warnings before taking action, and implement controls to detect and block malicious content or phishing attempts.

In summary, understanding the psychological principles exploited by social engineering attackers is crucial for developing effective security awareness programs, implementing robust security controls, and mitigating the risks posed by social engineering attacks. By educating employees about common manipulation techniques, promoting skepticism towards unsolicited messages or requests, and implementing security controls to detect and block malicious content, organizations can reduce the likelihood of successful social engineering attacks and protect against potential security breaches or data compromises.

Social engineering countermeasures are essential components of an organization's cybersecurity strategy, aimed at mitigating the risks posed by social engineering attacks and enhancing overall resilience against cyber threats. One fundamental countermeasure against social engineering attacks is user education and awareness training, which involves educating employees about common social engineering tactics, manipulation techniques, and red flags to recognize and respond to potential threats effectively. User education programs should cover topics such as phishing awareness, password security, secure communication practices, and the importance of verifying the legitimacy of requests or messages before disclosing sensitive information. Organizations can conduct regular security awareness training sessions, distribute informative materials and resources, and simulate social engineering scenarios to test employees' awareness and readiness to detect and respond to social engineering attacks effectively.

Furthermore, implementing strict access controls and user authentication mechanisms is crucial for preventing unauthorized access to sensitive information and resources, reducing the risk of social engineering attacks targeting privileged accounts or administrative credentials. Access control measures, such as role-based access control (RBAC), least privilege principle, and multi-factor authentication (MFA), can help organizations limit users' access rights based on their roles and responsibilities, minimize the potential impact of compromised accounts, and prevent unauthorized access to critical systems or data. Organizations can use the passwd command in Unix/Linux systems to manage user passwords, enforce password complexity requirements, and periodically rotate passwords to mitigate the risk of credential-based social engineering attacks.

Moreover, implementing email filtering and spam detection solutions is essential for detecting and blocking malicious content, phishing emails, and other social engineering attacks delivered via email. Email filtering solutions use various techniques, such as blacklisting, whitelisting, content analysis, and heuristic scanning, to identify and quarantine suspicious emails containing malicious attachments, links, or content. Organizations can deploy email filtering solutions, such as Microsoft Exchange Online Protection (EOP), Proofpoint, or Cisco Email Security, to filter incoming and outgoing emails, detect phishing attempts, and protect users from falling victim to social engineering attacks delivered via email. Additionally, organizations can configure email security settings to block external emails from suspicious or untrusted domains, scan attachments for malware, and flag phishing emails with warning banners or notifications to alert users about potential threats.

Furthermore, conducting regular security assessments and vulnerability scans can help organizations identify and address security weaknesses, misconfigurations, or vulnerabilities that could be exploited by social engineering attackers to gain unauthorized access or compromise systems. Security assessments, such as penetration testing, vulnerability scanning, and security audits, can help organizations identify gaps in their security posture, assess the effectiveness of existing controls, and prioritize remediation efforts to address critical vulnerabilities or weaknesses. Organizations can use vulnerability scanning tools, such as Nessus, Qualys, or OpenVAS, to scan their network infrastructure, systems, and applications for known vulnerabilities, misconfigurations, or weaknesses that could be exploited by attackers. Additionally, organizations can conduct social engineering penetration tests to assess employees' susceptibility to social engineering attacks, identify areas for improvement, and reinforce security awareness training programs.

Moreover, implementing security controls to detect and block malicious activities, such as intrusion detection and prevention systems (IDPS), can help organizations identify and mitigate social engineering attacks in real-time by monitoring network traffic, detecting suspicious behavior, and blocking malicious activities before they cause harm. IDPS solutions use signature-based detection, anomaly detection, and behavioral analysis techniques to identify and block known threats, zero-day attacks, and malicious behaviors indicative of social engineering attacks. Organizations can deploy IDPS solutions, such as Snort, Suricata, or Cisco Firepower, to monitor network traffic, analyze packet payloads, and detect common attack patterns or indicators of compromise associated with social engineering attacks. Additionally, organizations can configure IDPS rules and policies to alert security teams about suspicious activities, block malicious traffic, or quarantine compromised systems to prevent further damage or unauthorized access.

Furthermore, implementing security awareness and incident response policies and procedures is essential for facilitating timely detection, response, and mitigation of social engineering attacks, minimizing the impact of security incidents, and restoring normal operations effectively. Security awareness policies should outline employees' responsibilities for reporting security incidents, suspicious activities, or potential social engineering threats to the appropriate authorities or incident response teams. Incident response procedures should define the steps to be followed in the event of a security incident, including incident identification, containment, eradication, recovery, and post-incident analysis. Organizations can develop incident response playbooks, conduct tabletop exercises, and establish communication channels to coordinate incident response efforts, gather forensic evidence, and communicate with stakeholders during security incidents. Additionally, organizations can implement security controls, such as data loss prevention (DLP) solutions, endpoint detection and response (EDR) tools, and security information and event management (SIEM) systems, to monitor, detect, and respond to security incidents proactively.

In summary, social engineering countermeasures are essential for protecting organizations against the growing threat of social engineering attacks, mitigating the risks posed by manipulation tactics, and enhancing overall cybersecurity resilience. By implementing user education and awareness training, strict access controls, email filtering and spam detection solutions, security assessments and vulnerability scans, intrusion detection and prevention systems, and security awareness and incident response policies and procedures, organizations can reduce the likelihood of successful social engineering attacks, minimize the impact of security incidents, and safeguard critical assets and information from unauthorized access or compromise.

Chapter 5: Advanced Persistent Threats (APTs)

The Advanced Persistent Threat (APT) lifecycle encompasses a series of stages and tactics used by sophisticated cyber adversaries to infiltrate, persist within, and exfiltrate data from targeted networks or organizations, posing significant challenges to cybersecurity defenders and traditional security measures. The APT lifecycle typically begins with the reconnaissance phase, where attackers gather information about the target organization, its infrastructure, employees, and security posture through open-source intelligence (OSINT) gathering, social engineering, or reconnaissance tools. Attackers may use tools such as Shodan or Nmap to scan for open ports, identify vulnerable services, and gather information about the target's external attack surface, enabling them to identify potential entry points or weaknesses to exploit. During the initial compromise phase, attackers exploit vulnerabilities in the target organization's systems or applications to gain unauthorized access to the network, establish a foothold, and deploy malicious payloads, such as backdoors, remote access trojans (RATs), or malware implants, to maintain persistence and evade detection.

The initial compromise phase may involve exploiting known vulnerabilities, zero-day exploits, or targeted phishing campaigns to deliver malicious payloads to targeted individuals or systems within the organization.

Attackers may use exploit frameworks such as Metasploit or Cobalt Strike to deliver and execute malicious payloads, exploit vulnerabilities, and establish command and control (C2) channels for communicating with compromised systems. Once inside the network, attackers move laterally to expand their foothold, escalate privileges, and gain access to additional systems or resources within the target environment. Attackers may use techniques such as password spraying, credential theft, or exploitation of misconfigured permissions to escalate privileges and move laterally across the network, seeking valuable assets or sensitive information to exfiltrate.

During the persistence phase, attackers establish persistence mechanisms to maintain access to compromised systems or networks over an extended period, enabling them to continue their operations and evade detection by security controls or incident response teams. Persistence mechanisms may include creating hidden user accounts, modifying system settings or registry keys, scheduling recurring tasks, or deploying rootkits or kernel-level implants to maintain stealth and resilience against system reboots or security updates. Attackers may use techniques such as registry persistence, scheduled tasks, or startup scripts to ensure that their malicious payloads are executed automatically upon system boot or user login, allowing them to maintain access and control over compromised systems.

As attackers continue to move laterally and escalate privileges within the network, they may exfiltrate sensitive data or intellectual property from compromised systems or network segments to achieve their objectives, whether financial gain, espionage, or sabotage. Data exfiltration techniques may involve compressing, encrypting, or obfuscating stolen data before transmitting it to external servers or command and control infrastructure controlled by the attackers. Attackers may use techniques such as data exfiltration over encrypted channels, DNS tunneling, or covert communication channels embedded within legitimate network traffic to evade detection by network security controls or data loss prevention (DLP) systems.

Throughout the APT lifecycle, attackers employ various evasion and obfuscation techniques to evade detection by security controls, malware analysis tools, or incident response teams, making it challenging for defenders to detect, analyze, and respond to their activities effectively. Evasion techniques may include using encryption, obfuscation, or anti-analysis techniques to conceal malicious payloads, modifying file attributes or timestamps to evade file-based detection mechanisms, or using living-off-the-land techniques to blend in with legitimate system processes or network traffic. Attackers may also leverage fileless malware, memory-resident implants, or polymorphic malware to evade traditional antivirus or endpoint detection and response (EDR) solutions, making it difficult for defenders to detect and mitigate their activities.

To detect and respond to APT attacks effectively, organizations must adopt a proactive cybersecurity posture, employing a combination of preventive, detective, and response measures to identify and mitigate threats at each stage of the APT lifecycle. Preventive measures may include patch management, vulnerability scanning, application whitelisting, and network segmentation to reduce the attack surface, mitigate known vulnerabilities, and prevent unauthorized access to critical systems or data. Detective measures may include network traffic analysis, endpoint monitoring, log analysis, and threat intelligence feeds to detect anomalous behavior, suspicious activities, or indicators of compromise (IOCs) associated with APT attacks.

Response measures may include incident response planning, tabletop exercises, and incident response playbooks to ensure a coordinated and effective response to security incidents, minimize the impact of breaches, and restore normal operations quickly. Additionally, organizations can leverage threat hunting techniques, such as proactive network and endpoint monitoring, behavioral analysis, and IOC hunting, to identify and mitigate APT threats before they cause significant damage or loss. By adopting a multi-layered approach to cybersecurity, organizations can enhance their resilience against APT attacks, detect and respond to threats effectively, and protect their critical assets and information from sophisticated cyber adversaries.

APT detection and mitigation strategies are essential components of a robust cybersecurity defense posture, aimed at identifying and neutralizing advanced persistent threats (APTs) before they can cause significant harm to an organization's systems, data, or reputation. One effective strategy for detecting APTs is the implementation of continuous monitoring and threat detection mechanisms across the organization's network infrastructure, endpoints, and cloud environments. Continuous monitoring involves the real-time collection, analysis, and correlation of security events and indicators of compromise (IOCs) from diverse sources, such as network traffic, system logs, endpoint telemetry, and threat intelligence feeds, to identify anomalous behavior, suspicious activities, or potential signs of APT activity.

Organizations can leverage security information and event management (SIEM) platforms, such as Splunk, LogRhythm, or Elastic SIEM, to aggregate and analyze security event data from various sources, correlate related events, and generate alerts or notifications for potential security incidents. SIEM solutions enable organizations to create custom detection rules, develop behavioral baselines, and automate response actions to detect and mitigate APT threats effectively. Additionally, organizations can deploy network intrusion detection systems (NIDS) and host-based intrusion detection systems (HIDS) to monitor network traffic, detect malicious activities, and alert security teams about potential APT attacks targeting the organization's infrastructure or endpoints.

Furthermore, organizations can enhance their APT detection capabilities by leveraging threat intelligence feeds, threat hunting techniques, and machine learning algorithms to identify emerging threats, advanced attack patterns, and indicators of compromise associated with APT campaigns. Threat intelligence feeds provide organizations with timely and relevant information about known APT groups, tactics, techniques, and procedures (TTPs), enabling them to proactively identify and respond to potential threats before they escalate into full-blown security incidents. Threat hunting involves proactively searching for signs of malicious activity or unauthorized access within the organization's network environment, using advanced analytics, behavioral analysis, and manual investigation techniques to uncover hidden threats or persistent adversaries.

Additionally, organizations can deploy endpoint detection and response (EDR) solutions, such as CrowdStrike Falcon, Carbon Black, or Microsoft Defender for Endpoint, to monitor and respond to suspicious activities, malicious behavior, and fileless attacks targeting endpoints across the organization's network. EDR solutions provide organizations with real-time visibility into endpoint activities, threat hunting capabilities, and automated response actions to detect and mitigate APT threats at the endpoint level. By deploying EDR solutions, organizations can detect and respond to APT attacks in real-time, contain the spread of malware or malicious activities, and minimize the impact of security incidents on their infrastructure and operations.

Moreover, organizations can strengthen their APT detection and mitigation capabilities by implementing network segmentation, least privilege access controls, and zero-trust security architectures to limit the lateral movement of attackers within the network and mitigate the risk of data exfiltration or unauthorized access to critical systems or resources. Network segmentation involves dividing the organization's network infrastructure into separate security zones or segments, such as internal, DMZ, and guest networks, and implementing access controls, firewalls, and intrusion prevention systems (IPS) to restrict traffic flow between segments and prevent attackers from moving laterally within the network.

Additionally, organizations can implement least privilege access controls to restrict users' access rights and permissions to the minimum level necessary to perform their job functions, reducing the risk of privilege escalation attacks and unauthorized access to sensitive data or systems. Zero-trust security architectures advocate for the principle of "never trust, always verify," whereby organizations assume that internal and external networks are compromised and implement strict access controls, identity verification mechanisms, and continuous monitoring to authenticate and authorize users, devices, and applications before granting access to resources or services.

Furthermore, organizations can enhance their APT detection and mitigation capabilities by conducting regular security assessments, penetration testing, and red team exercises to identify weaknesses, vulnerabilities, and gaps in their security posture and simulate real-world APT scenarios to test their detection and response capabilities. Security assessments involve evaluating the effectiveness of existing security controls, policies, and procedures, identifying areas for improvement, and prioritizing remediation efforts to address critical vulnerabilities or weaknesses. Penetration testing involves simulating APT attacks and exploitation techniques to identify potential entry points, privilege escalation paths, and data exfiltration opportunities within the organization's network environment.

Red team exercises involve emulating sophisticated adversaries and advanced attack scenarios to assess the organization's detection and response capabilities, validate security controls, and identify areas for improvement in the organization's incident response procedures, threat intelligence sharing, and collaboration among security teams. By conducting regular security assessments, penetration testing, and red team exercises, organizations can identify and mitigate APT threats effectively, improve their security posture, and enhance their resilience against advanced cyber threats.

Chapter 6: Recognizing Insider Threats

Insider threat indicators are behavioral, technical, or situational signs that may suggest an insider poses a risk to an organization's security, integrity, or confidentiality. These indicators can vary widely depending on the nature of the insider threat and the individual's motives, intentions, and access to sensitive information or systems. Behavioral indicators of insider threats may include changes in an employee's work patterns, performance, or behavior, such as sudden changes in work hours, frequent access to unauthorized areas or systems, or unusual levels of network activity outside of normal business hours. Additionally, disgruntled employees, individuals experiencing financial difficulties, or those with a history of conflicts with colleagues or supervisors may exhibit behaviors indicative of potential insider threats, such as expressing negative sentiments toward the organization, displaying aggressive behavior, or exhibiting signs of stress or dissatisfaction.

Technical indicators of insider threats may include unauthorized access to sensitive data or systems, suspicious file transfers or downloads, or the installation of unauthorized software or applications on company devices. Organizations can use endpoint monitoring tools, such as Sysinternals Process Monitor, Windows Event Viewer, or File Integrity Monitoring (FIM) solutions, to track and log user activities, file access events, and system changes to identify suspicious behavior or unauthorized activities that may indicate an insider threat. Additionally, organizations can leverage user and entity behavior analytics (UEBA) platforms, such as Splunk User Behavior Analytics or Exabeam, to analyze user behavior, detect anomalous activities, and identify potential insider threats based on deviations from established baselines or patterns of normal behavior.

Situational indicators of insider threats may include employees accessing sensitive information or systems outside of their normal job responsibilities or business requirements, attempting to bypass security controls or circumvent access restrictions, or exhibiting signs of stress, dissatisfaction, or personal crisis that may affect their judgment or decision-making abilities. Organizations can establish clear security policies and procedures, conduct regular security awareness training, and promote a culture of security awareness and vigilance among employees to help identify and report suspicious activities or behaviors that may indicate potential insider threats. Additionally, organizations can implement user activity monitoring, data loss prevention (DLP) solutions, and access controls to monitor and restrict employees' access to sensitive data or systems based on their roles, responsibilities, and business needs.

Insider threat indicators may also manifest in the form of unusual or unexplained financial transactions, such as employees making large purchases or withdrawals, engaging in unauthorized financial activities, or displaying signs of financial distress that may indicate potential involvement in malicious activities or fraud schemes. Organizations can monitor financial transactions, conduct regular audits of financial records, and implement fraud detection and prevention controls to identify and mitigate insider threats related to financial misconduct or embezzlement. Additionally, organizations can establish whistleblower programs, anonymous reporting channels, and mechanisms for employees to report suspected insider threats or unethical behavior without fear of retaliation, facilitating early detection and intervention before potential threats escalate into security incidents or breaches.

Furthermore, organizations can leverage data analytics, machine learning, and artificial intelligence (AI) technologies to analyze vast amounts of data, identify patterns, trends, and anomalies, and detect potential insider threats based on behavioral patterns, historical data, and predictive modeling techniques. By combining behavioral analytics, threat intelligence, and data mining capabilities, organizations can enhance their ability to detect, investigate, and mitigate insider threats in real-time, minimizing the impact of security incidents and safeguarding sensitive information and assets from insider abuse or exploitation. Additionally, organizations can establish insider threat detection and response teams, comprising cross-functional stakeholders from IT, security, human resources, legal, and compliance departments, to collaborate on identifying, investigating, and mitigating insider threats effectively.

In summary, insider threat indicators play a critical role in helping organizations detect, investigate, and mitigate risks posed by insiders with malicious intent or unauthorized access to sensitive information or systems. By monitoring behavioral, technical, and situational indicators of insider threats, implementing security controls and monitoring solutions, promoting a culture of security awareness and vigilance, and leveraging advanced analytics and AI technologies, organizations can strengthen their defenses against insider threats and protect their assets, reputation, and intellectual property from insider abuse or exploitation.

Insider threat prevention measures are critical components of an organization's cybersecurity strategy, aimed at mitigating the risks posed by trusted insiders who may intentionally or unintentionally compromise the organization's security, integrity, or confidentiality. One effective prevention measure is the implementation of robust access control policies and procedures to limit employees' access to sensitive data, systems, and resources based on their roles, responsibilities, and business needs. Organizations can use access control mechanisms, such as role-based access control (RBAC), attribute-based access control (ABAC), or mandatory access control (MAC), to enforce least privilege principles and restrict employees' access to only the information and systems necessary to perform their job functions.

Additionally, organizations can implement user authentication and authorization mechanisms, such as multi-factor authentication (MFA), strong passwords, and biometric authentication, to verify users' identities and prevent unauthorized access to sensitive information or systems. By requiring users to authenticate themselves using multiple factors, such as passwords, biometrics, or security tokens, organizations can enhance their security posture and reduce the risk of insider threats resulting from compromised credentials or unauthorized access to privileged accounts. Organizations can deploy authentication solutions, such as Microsoft Azure Active Directory, Duo Security, or RSA SecurID, to enforce MFA and strengthen access controls across their network infrastructure and cloud services.

Furthermore, organizations can establish clear security policies and procedures, outlining acceptable use of company resources, data handling practices, and employee responsibilities for safeguarding sensitive information and systems from insider threats. Security policies should define acceptable behaviors, security requirements, and consequences for policy violations, providing employees with clear guidance on their roles and responsibilities in maintaining the organization's security posture. Additionally, organizations can conduct regular security awareness training and education programs to educate employees about the risks of insider threats, common attack vectors, and best practices for identifying and reporting suspicious activities or behaviors.

Another prevention measure is the implementation of data loss prevention (DLP) solutions to monitor, detect, and prevent unauthorized disclosure of sensitive data or intellectual property by insiders. DLP solutions use policy-based rules and content inspection techniques to identify and classify sensitive data, monitor data flows, and prevent data leakage or exfiltration through email, web uploads, removable storage devices, or cloud applications. Organizations can deploy DLP solutions, such as Symantec Data Loss Prevention, McAfee Total Protection for Data Loss Prevention, or Microsoft Information Protection, to enforce data security policies, monitor user activities, and protect sensitive information from insider threats.

Moreover, organizations can implement insider threat detection and monitoring solutions to proactively identify and mitigate suspicious activities, behaviors, or anomalies that may indicate potential insider threats. Insider threat detection solutions use advanced analytics, machine learning, and behavioral modeling techniques to analyze user behavior, network traffic, system logs, and other sources of security telemetry to identify patterns of activity indicative of insider threats. Organizations can deploy insider threat detection solutions, such as ObserveIT, Varonis Insider Threat Detection, or Securonix UEBA, to monitor user activities, detect anomalies, and generate alerts or notifications for potential insider threats.

Additionally, organizations can establish incident response plans and procedures to facilitate a coordinated and effective response to insider threats, ensuring that security incidents are promptly identified, investigated, and remediated to minimize the impact on the organization's operations and reputation. Incident response plans should outline roles and responsibilities, escalation procedures, communication protocols, and mitigation strategies for responding to insider threats, enabling organizations to respond swiftly and effectively to security incidents involving insiders. By establishing incident response capabilities, organizations can mitigate the impact of insider threats, contain security incidents, and prevent further damage to their assets, reputation, and business operations.

In summary, insider threat prevention measures are essential for safeguarding organizations against the risks posed by trusted insiders with access to sensitive information or systems. By implementing access control policies, user authentication mechanisms, security awareness training programs, DLP solutions, insider threat detection solutions, and incident response capabilities, organizations can mitigate the risks of insider threats, protect their assets and intellectual property, and maintain the integrity, confidentiality, and availability of their systems and data.

Chapter 7: Analyzing Threat Intelligence Feeds

Threat intelligence gathering techniques encompass a variety of methods and tools used by cybersecurity professionals to collect, analyze, and disseminate information about potential threats, vulnerabilities, and malicious actors targeting organizations' systems, networks, and data. One common technique is open-source intelligence (OSINT), which involves gathering information from publicly available sources, such as websites, social media platforms, forums, and news articles, to identify potential threats, vulnerabilities, or indicators of compromise (IOCs). Security analysts can use OSINT tools, such as Maltego, Shodan, or SpiderFoot, to search for information about domain names, IP addresses, email addresses, and other digital artifacts associated with potential threats or malicious activities.

Additionally, organizations can leverage threat intelligence feeds and information-sharing platforms to obtain real-time information about emerging threats, attack patterns, and malicious infrastructure used by threat actors. Threat intelligence feeds provide organizations with timely and relevant data about known threats, vulnerabilities, and indicators of compromise (IOCs), enabling them to proactively identify and respond to potential security incidents before they escalate into full-blown breaches. Organizations can subscribe to commercial threat intelligence feeds from vendors such as Recorded Future, Anomali, or ThreatConnect, or participate in information-sharing communities, such as the Information Sharing and Analysis Centers (ISACs) or the Cyber Threat Alliance (CTA), to exchange threat intelligence with other organizations and industry peers. Furthermore, organizations can conduct reconnaissance and scanning activities to gather information about their own systems, networks, and assets from an attacker's perspective, identifying potential attack vectors, misconfigurations, or weaknesses that could be exploited by threat actors. Security professionals can use network scanning tools, such as Nmap, Nessus, or OpenVAS, to discover devices, services, and open ports on their networks, assess vulnerabilities, and prioritize remediation efforts based on the severity of identified issues. Additionally, organizations can deploy honeypots, decoy systems, or network sensors to lure attackers into controlled environments, gather information about their tactics, techniques, and procedures (TTPs), and enhance their understanding of emerging threats and attack trends.

Moreover, organizations can monitor and analyze dark web forums, marketplaces, and underground communities frequented by cybercriminals to gather intelligence about potential threats, new attack techniques, and compromised credentials or data for sale. Security researchers can use specialized tools, such as DarkOwl Vision, Recorded Future, or Cybersixgill, to monitor dark web forums, analyze chatter, and identify discussions related to specific organizations, industries, or attack campaigns. By monitoring the dark web, organizations can gain insights into emerging threats, targeted attacks, and cybercriminal activities that may pose a risk to their assets, reputation, or operations.

Additionally, organizations can conduct phishing simulations and social engineering tests to assess employees' susceptibility to phishing attacks, identify areas for improvement in security awareness training programs, and gather intelligence about potential insider threats or weaknesses in their security posture. Security teams can use phishing simulation platforms, such as KnowBe4, PhishMe, or Cofense PhishMe, to create and launch simulated phishing campaigns, track user responses, and measure the effectiveness of security awareness training efforts. Furthermore, organizations can analyze phishing emails, malicious attachments, or URLs collected during simulations to identify common phishing techniques, trends, and tactics used by attackers to trick users into disclosing sensitive information or downloading malware.

Furthermore, organizations can leverage threat hunting techniques to proactively search for signs of malicious activity or unauthorized access within their network environments, using advanced analytics, behavioral analysis, and threat intelligence to uncover hidden threats or persistent adversaries. Threat hunters can use data analytics platforms, such as Elasticsearch, Splunk, or IBM QRadar, to analyze large volumes of security telemetry, identify anomalous behavior, and prioritize investigation efforts based on the severity of potential threats. Additionally, organizations can establish threat hunting teams, comprising skilled analysts, incident responders, and threat intelligence experts, to collaborate on identifying, investigating, and mitigating potential threats in real-time.

In summary, threat intelligence gathering techniques play a crucial role in helping organizations identify, assess, and mitigate cybersecurity risks, enabling them to stay ahead of emerging threats and protect their systems, networks, and data from malicious actors. By leveraging open-source intelligence (OSINT), threat intelligence feeds, reconnaissance and scanning activities, dark web monitoring, phishing simulations, social engineering tests, and threat hunting techniques, organizations can gather valuable insights into potential threats, vulnerabilities, and attack trends, enabling them to make informed decisions and take proactive measures to enhance their security posture and resilience against cyber threats.

Threat intelligence analysis frameworks provide structured methodologies and processes for analyzing and synthesizing threat intelligence data to identify, assess, and prioritize potential threats, vulnerabilities, and risks facing an organization's systems, networks, and data. One commonly used framework is the Cyber Kill Chain, developed by Lockheed Martin, which describes the stages of a cyber attack, from initial reconnaissance and weaponization to exfiltration and impact, enabling organizations to identify and disrupt attacks at each stage of the kill chain. Security analysts can use the Cyber Kill Chain framework to analyze threat intelligence data, map observed attacker behaviors to specific stages of the kill chain, and develop countermeasures and mitigations to thwart attacks before they reach their objectives.

Another widely adopted framework is the Diamond Model of Intrusion Analysis, which provides a structured approach for analyzing cyber threats based on four key components: adversary, infrastructure, capabilities, and victim. Security analysts can use the Diamond Model to correlate observed indicators of compromise (IOCs) with known adversary tactics, techniques, and procedures (TTPs), identify patterns of malicious activity, and attribute attacks to specific threat actors or groups based on their infrastructure, capabilities, and targeting preferences. Additionally, the Diamond Model enables organizations to assess the impact of cyber threats on their operations, prioritize response efforts, and develop tailored mitigation strategies to defend against future attacks.

Furthermore, the MITRE ATT&CK framework is a comprehensive knowledge base of adversary tactics, techniques, and procedures (TTPs) organized into a matrix of attack techniques and sub-techniques, enabling organizations to map observed behaviors to specific adversary tactics and enhance their understanding of attacker tradecraft. Security analysts can use the MITRE ATT&CK framework to analyze threat intelligence data, identify common attack patterns, and assess the effectiveness of existing security controls in detecting and preventing known adversary techniques. Additionally, organizations can use the MITRE ATT&CK

framework to develop threat-informed defense strategies, prioritize security investments, and improve their resilience against evolving cyber threats.

Moreover, the Structured Threat Information eXpression (STIX) and Trusted Automated eXchange of Indicator Information (TAXII) are industry standards developed by the Cyber Threat Intelligence (CTI) community for sharing, exchanging, and collaborating on threat intelligence data in a standardized format. STIX provides a common language for describing cyber threats, indicators of compromise (IOCs), and threat actors, while TAXII enables organizations to exchange threat intelligence data with trusted partners, government agencies, and industry peers in real-time. By leveraging STIX and TAXII, organizations can improve their situational awareness, collaborate on threat intelligence sharing, and automate the ingestion and analysis of threat data from multiple sources.

Additionally, the Diamond Model for Intrusion Analysis (DMA) is an extension of the Diamond Model that incorporates additional dimensions, such as time, space, and relationships, to provide a more holistic view of cyber threats and adversary behaviors. DMA enables organizations to analyze the temporal and spatial aspects of cyber attacks, track adversary movements and interactions across different attack campaigns, and identify patterns of behavior indicative of advanced persistent threats (APTs) or sophisticated cyber adversaries. Furthermore, DMA facilitates threat hunting and intelligence-driven defense by enabling organizations to correlate disparate pieces of threat intelligence data, identify common attack patterns, and develop proactive detection and response strategies to mitigate cyber threats effectively.

In summary, threat intelligence analysis frameworks provide organizations with structured methodologies and processes for analyzing, synthesizing, and operationalizing threat intelligence data to enhance their understanding of cyber threats and improve their resilience against evolving security risks. By leveraging frameworks such as the Cyber Kill Chain, Diamond Model of Intrusion Analysis, MITRE ATT&CK framework, STIX, TAXII, and DMA, organizations can identify, assess, and prioritize threats, develop tailored mitigation strategies, and enhance their ability to detect, respond to, and recover from cyber attacks in a timely and effective manner.

Chapter 8: Incident Response Strategies

Incident response planning and preparation are critical components of an organization's cybersecurity strategy, aimed at ensuring a timely and effective response to security incidents, minimizing their impact on business operations, and mitigating the risk of data breaches or unauthorized access to sensitive information. One key aspect of incident response planning is the development of an incident response plan (IRP), which outlines the procedures, roles, responsibilities, and communication protocols for responding to security incidents in a coordinated and systematic manner. Security teams can use templates or guidelines, such as those provided by the National Institute of Standards and Technology (NIST) or the International Organization for Standardization (ISO), to develop customized IRPs tailored to their organization's specific needs and requirements.

Moreover, organizations can establish incident response teams comprising skilled professionals from various disciplines, including cybersecurity, IT operations, legal, human resources, and public relations, to collaborate on Incident response activities and ensure a comprehensive and coordinated approach to managing security incidents. Incident response teams should have clearly defined roles and responsibilities, designated points of contact, and predefined escalation procedures to facilitate communication and decision-making during security incidents. Additionally, organizations can conduct regular training exercises, tabletop simulations, or incident response drills to test the effectiveness of their IRPs, validate the readiness of their incident response teams, and identify areas for improvement in their incident response capabilities.

Furthermore, organizations can implement incident detection and monitoring capabilities to detect and alert on suspicious activities, anomalies, or indicators of compromise (IOCs) that may indicate a security incident or breach. Security teams can use security information and event management (SIEM) platforms, intrusion detection systems (IDS), endpoint detection and response (EDR) solutions, or network traffic analysis (NTA) tools to monitor network traffic, system logs, and user activities for signs of malicious activity or unauthorized access. Additionally, organizations can deploy security orchestration, automation, and response (SOAR) solutions to automate incident detection, triage, and response processes, enabling them to respond rapidly to security incidents and mitigate their impact on business operations.

Moreover, organizations can establish incident response playbooks, which document predefined response procedures, decision trees, and workflows for specific types of security incidents, such as malware infections, data breaches, or denial-of-service (DoS) attacks. Incident response playbooks provide security teams with step-by-step instructions and best practices for containing, investigating, and remedying security incidents, ensuring consistency and efficiency in their incident response efforts. Additionally, organizations can develop incident response runbooks, which contain detailed technical procedures, commands, and checklists for executing specific incident response tasks, such as isolating infected systems, collecting forensic evidence, or restoring backups.

Additionally, organizations can establish relationships with external partners, such as incident response service providers, law enforcement agencies, regulatory authorities, and industry peers, to enhance their incident response capabilities and access additional resources and expertise during security incidents. Incident response service providers can offer specialized expertise, technical assistance, and incident response support to help organizations effectively manage and remediate security incidents, while law enforcement agencies and regulatory authorities can provide guidance, legal assistance, and coordination support during incident response activities. Moreover, organizations can participate in information-sharing and collaboration initiatives, such as information sharing and analysis centers (ISACs) or threat intelligence sharing communities, to exchange threat intelligence, share best practices, and collaborate on incident response activities with other organizations in their industry or sector.

Furthermore, organizations can leverage incident response management platforms or incident tracking systems to facilitate the coordination, documentation, and tracking of incident response activities, enabling them to capture critical information, maintain an audit trail of actions taken, and generate reports for post-incident analysis and review. Incident response management platforms provide centralized dashboards, case management capabilities, and workflow automation features to streamline incident response processes, improve communication and collaboration among incident response teams, and ensure compliance with regulatory requirements and internal policies. Additionally, incident tracking systems enable organizations to categorize, prioritize, and track the status of security incidents, assign tasks to relevant stakeholders, and monitor progress towards resolution.

In summary, incident response planning and preparation are essential for enabling organizations to effectively detect, respond to, and recover from security incidents, ensuring the continuity of business operations and minimizing the impact of cyber threats on their systems, networks, and data. By developing incident response plans, establishing incident response teams, implementing incident detection and monitoring capabilities, creating incident response playbooks and runbooks, building relationships with external partners, and leveraging incident response management platforms, organizations can enhance their incident response capabilities, improve their resilience against cyber threats, and protect their assets, reputation, and stakeholders' trust.

Incident containment and eradication techniques are critical components of an organization's incident response process, aimed at preventing further spread of a security incident and removing any malicious presence from the affected systems or networks. One key technique for incident containment is network segmentation, which involves dividing a network into separate subnetworks or segments to contain the spread of a security incident and limit the potential impact on other parts of the network. Security teams can use network infrastructure devices, such as routers, switches, and firewalls, to implement access control lists (ACLs) or virtual LANs (VLANs) to restrict traffic flow between network segments and prevent lateral movement by attackers.

Moreover, organizations can deploy endpoint protection solutions, such as antivirus software, endpoint detection and response (EDR) tools, or host-based intrusion prevention systems (HIPS), to contain the spread of malware and prevent it from infecting other endpoints on the network. Security teams can use these endpoint protection solutions to quarantine infected devices, isolate them from the network, and remediate security vulnerabilities or misconfigurations that may have contributed to the incident. Additionally, organizations can leverage endpoint isolation techniques, such as network access control (NAC) or port-based access control, to restrict network access for compromised endpoints and prevent them from communicating with other devices on the network.

Furthermore, organizations can implement network-based intrusion detection and prevention systems (IDS/IPS) to detect and block malicious network traffic associated with security incidents, such as denial-of-service (DoS) attacks, malware downloads, or command-and-control (C2) communications. Security teams can configure IDS/IPS rules or signatures to identify known attack patterns or anomalous behavior and automatically block or alert on suspicious traffic in real-time. Additionally, organizations can use threat intelligence feeds or threat hunting techniques to identify indicators of compromise (IOCs) or advanced persistent threats (APTs) and proactively block or mitigate them using firewall rules or network access control lists (ACLs).

Moreover, organizations can leverage log management and security information and event management (SIEM) platforms to collect, correlate, and analyze log data from various sources, such as network devices, servers, applications, and security tools, to identify anomalous behavior or security incidents. Security teams can use SIEM platforms to create alerts, dashboards, and reports that provide visibility into security events, facilitate incident response coordination, and enable rapid decision-making during security incidents. Additionally, organizations can automate incident response actions, such as quarantining infected devices, blocking malicious IP addresses, or disabling compromised user accounts, using orchestration and automation tools integrated with their SIEM platform.

Furthermore, organizations can conduct forensic analysis and digital investigations to gather evidence, identify the root cause of a security incident, and determine the extent of the impact on their systems, networks, and data. Security teams can use forensic tools, such as EnCase, FTK, or Volatility, to collect and analyze forensic artifacts, such as system logs, memory dumps, and file system metadata, to reconstruct the timeline of events leading up to and following a security incident. Additionally, organizations can preserve evidence in a forensically sound manner, document their findings, and prepare reports for internal review, regulatory compliance, or legal proceedings. Additionally, organizations can leverage threat intelligence feeds or threat hunting techniques to identify indicators of compromise (IOCs) or advanced persistent threats (APTs) and proactively block or mitigate them using firewall rules or network access control lists (ACLs). Moreover, organizations can implement security controls, such as intrusion detection and prevention systems (IDPS), web application firewalls (WAFs), or data loss prevention (DLP) solutions, to detect and block malicious activities, such as unauthorized access attempts, data exfiltration, or exploitation of software vulnerabilities.

In summary, incident containment and eradication techniques are essential for minimizing the impact of security incidents, restoring the integrity of affected systems, and preventing future incidents from occurring. By implementing network segmentation, endpoint protection solutions, network-based IDS/IPS, log management and SIEM platforms, orchestration and automation tools, forensic analysis techniques, and proactive threat intelligence-driven security controls, organizations can effectively contain and eradicate security incidents, protect their assets and data, and maintain the confidentiality, integrity, and availability of their systems and networks.

Chapter 9: Threat Hunting Techniques

Threat hunting methodologies are proactive approaches used by cybersecurity teams to detect and mitigate potential threats that may have evaded traditional security measures. One widely used threat hunting methodology is the Cyber Kill Chain, which is based on the premise that cyber attacks follow a series of stages, from initial reconnaissance to data exfiltration, enabling organizations to identify and disrupt attacks at various stages of the kill chain. Security analysts can leverage the Cyber Kill Chain framework to analyze security logs, network traffic, and endpoint telemetry data for indicators of compromise (IOCs) or anomalous behavior indicative of ongoing attacks.

Moreover, organizations can implement the Diamond Model of Intrusion Analysis, which provides a structured approach for analyzing cyber threats based on four key components: adversary, infrastructure, capabilities, and victim. Security analysts can use the Diamond Model to correlate observed IOCs with known adversary tactics, techniques, and procedures (TTPs), identify patterns of malicious activity, and attribute attacks to specific threat actors or groups. Additionally, organizations can conduct threat hunting exercises using the Diamond Model to proactively search for signs of adversary presence or intent in their network environments.

Furthermore, the MITRE ATT&CK framework is a comprehensive knowledge base of adversary tactics, techniques, and procedures (TTPs) organized into a matrix of attack techniques and sub-techniques, enabling organizations to map observed behaviors to specific adversary tactics and enhance their understanding of attacker tradecraft. Security analysts can use the MITRE ATT&CK framework to guide their threat hunting activities, identify common attack patterns, and assess the effectiveness of existing security controls in detecting and preventing known adversary techniques. Additionally, organizations can develop custom threat hunting playbooks based on the MITRE ATT&CK framework to target specific adversary tactics and prioritize their threat hunting efforts.

Moreover, organizations can leverage threat intelligence feeds, open-source intelligence (OSINT), and industry-specific threat intelligence reports to enrich their understanding of emerging threats, adversary behaviors, and attack trends relevant to their industry or sector. Security analysts can use threat intelligence data to identify potential threat actors, their tactics, techniques, and procedures (TTPs), and indicators of compromise (IOCs) associated with known threat campaigns. Additionally, organizations can integrate threat intelligence feeds into their threat hunting processes to prioritize high-risk threats, validate security alerts, and enrich their detection capabilities with external context.

Furthermore, organizations can deploy network traffic analysis (NTA) tools, endpoint detection and response (EDR) solutions, and security information and event management (SIEM) platforms to collect, correlate, and analyze telemetry data from various sources, such as network devices, endpoints, and security tools. Security analysts can use these tools to identify anomalous behavior, suspicious patterns, or indicators of compromise (IOCs) that may indicate a security incident or breach. Additionally, organizations can leverage machine learning and behavioral analytics algorithms to detect subtle signs of malicious activity and uncover previously unknown threats.

Additionally, organizations can conduct threat hunting exercises using a hypothesis-driven approach, where security analysts formulate hypotheses or assumptions about potential threats based on their knowledge of attacker tactics, techniques, and procedures (TTPs), and then test these hypotheses by analyzing security data and telemetry from their network environment. Security analysts can use techniques such as data mining, pattern recognition, and statistical analysis to identify deviations from normal behavior, identify outliers, and uncover signs of potential threats. Moreover, organizations can leverage threat hunting platforms or tools that provide automated workflows, analytics, and visualization capabilities to streamline their threat hunting processes, improve efficiency, and scale their threat hunting operations across large and complex environments.

In summary, threat hunting methodologies are essential for organizations to proactively detect and mitigate potential threats that may evade traditional security measures. By leveraging frameworks such as the Cyber Kill Chain, Diamond Model of Intrusion Analysis, MITRE

ATT&CK framework, threat intelligence feeds, and hypothesis-driven threat hunting approaches, organizations can enhance their threat detection capabilities, improve their understanding of adversary behaviors, and strengthen their overall cybersecurity posture. Moreover, by deploying advanced analytics tools, machine learning algorithms, and automation capabilities, organizations can streamline their threat hunting processes, reduce response times, and effectively defend against emerging cyber threats.

Threat hunting tools and technologies play a crucial role in enabling cybersecurity teams to proactively detect and respond to potential threats within their network environments. One widely used tool in threat hunting is the Security Information and Event Management (SIEM) platform, which aggregates and correlates security event data from various sources, such as network devices, servers, and endpoints, to provide centralized visibility into potential security incidents. Security analysts can use SIEM platforms to create custom rules and alerts based on known attack patterns or suspicious behavior, allowing them to quickly identify and investigate potential threats.

Additionally, organizations can leverage Endpoint Detection and Response (EDR) solutions to monitor and analyze endpoint telemetry data for signs of malicious activity or unauthorized behavior. EDR solutions provide real-time visibility into endpoint activities, including process executions, file modifications, and network connections, enabling security teams to detect and respond to threats at the endpoint level. Security analysts can use EDR platforms to conduct forensic analysis, quarantine infected endpoints, and remediate security incidents to prevent further damage.

Moreover, Network Traffic Analysis (NTA) tools are essential for identifying anomalous network behavior and potential security threats. NTA solutions analyze network traffic patterns, protocols, and communications to detect suspicious activities, such as lateral movement, data exfiltration, or command-and-control (C2) communications. Security analysts can use NTA platforms to monitor network traffic in real-time, identify deviations from normal behavior, and investigate potential security incidents.

Furthermore, organizations can deploy Threat Intelligence Platforms (TIPs) to aggregate, enrich, and analyze threat intelligence data from various sources, such as commercial feeds, open-source intelligence (OSINT), and internal sources. TIPs provide security teams with contextual information about known threats, adversary tactics, and indicators of compromise (IOCs), enabling them to prioritize their threat hunting efforts and respond to emerging threats effectively. Security analysts can use TIPs to correlate threat intelligence data with security events and telemetry from their network environment to identify potential threats and take proactive measures to mitigate them.

Additionally, organizations can leverage open-source threat hunting tools and frameworks, such as HELK (Hunting ELK), Sigma, and MISP (Malware Information Sharing Platform), to enhance their threat hunting capabilities without incurring significant costs. These tools provide security analysts with pre-built queries, rules, and playbooks for conducting threat hunting activities, enabling them to quickly identify and respond to potential threats. Moreover, organizations can contribute to and benefit from the collective knowledge and expertise of the cybersecurity community by participating in threat intelligence sharing platforms and communities, such as ISACs (Information Sharing and Analysis Centers) or threat intelligence sharing consortia.

Moreover, organizations can deploy Security Orchestration, Automation, and Response (SOAR) platforms to streamline their threat hunting processes, automate repetitive tasks, and orchestrate incident response workflows. SOAR platforms integrate with existing security tools and technologies to aggregate security alerts, prioritize incidents, and automate response actions based on predefined playbooks or workflows. Security analysts can use SOAR platforms to accelerate threat detection and response, reduce response times, and improve overall security posture.

Additionally, organizations can leverage Machine Learning (ML) and Artificial Intelligence (AI) technologies to augment their threat hunting capabilities and improve detection accuracy. ML and AI algorithms can analyze large volumes of security data, identify patterns, and detect subtle signs of malicious activity that may evade traditional signature-based detection methods. Security teams can use ML and AI-powered analytics platforms to uncover unknown threats, prioritize high-risk alerts, and enhance their ability to detect and respond to emerging cyber threats. Furthermore, organizations can conduct tabletop exercises and red team simulations to test their threat hunting capabilities, validate their incident response procedures, and improve their readiness to handle real-world security incidents. Tabletop exercises involve scenario-based discussions and role-playing exercises to simulate various cyber threats and evaluate the effectiveness of the organization's response plans. Red team simulations involve adversarial simulations conducted by internal or external security teams to mimic the tactics, techniques, and procedures (TTPs) of real-world threat actors and assess the organization's defensive capabilities.

In summary, threat hunting tools and technologies are essential for organizations to proactively detect and respond to potential security threats within their network environments. By leveraging SIEM platforms, EDR solutions, NTA tools, TIPs, open-source threat hunting tools, SOAR platforms, ML/AI analytics, and tabletop exercises, organizations can enhance their threat hunting capabilities, improve detection accuracy, and strengthen their overall cybersecurity posture. Moreover, by continuously evolving their threat hunting strategies and leveraging emerging technologies, organizations can stay ahead of evolving cyber threats and effectively defend against advanced adversaries.

Chapter 10: Forensic Investigation Methods

Digital forensics fundamentals encompass a broad range of techniques, methodologies, and tools used to investigate and analyze digital evidence related to cybercrimes and security incidents. One of the key principles of digital forensics is the preservation of evidence integrity, which involves maintaining the integrity, authenticity, and confidentiality of digital evidence throughout the investigation process. To achieve this, forensic investigators employ a variety of techniques, such as creating forensic images of storage devices using tools like dd or FTK Imager, which create bit-by-bit copies of disk drives or partitions, ensuring that the original evidence remains unchanged. These forensic images serve as a pristine copy of the original storage media and are used for analysis and examination without altering the original evidence.

Moreover, digital forensic investigators rely on a variety of forensic analysis techniques to examine digital evidence and extract relevant information. One such technique is file system analysis, which involves analyzing the structure and metadata of file systems to identify files, directories, and artifacts related to a security incident or cybercrime. Tools like The Sleuth Kit (TSK) and Autopsy provide capabilities for file system analysis, enabling investigators to recover deleted files, extract file metadata, and reconstruct file relationships to reconstruct the sequence of events leading to the incident Additionally, memory forensics is another essential aspect of digital forensics, focusing on the analysis of volatile memory (RAM) to identify running processes, network connections, and artifacts related to malicious activities. Memory forensics tools like Volatility Framework enable investigators to extract valuable information from memory dumps, such as process memory, registry hives, and network socket connections, allowing them to uncover evidence of malware execution, rootkit presence, or unauthorized access to sensitive data.

Furthermore, network forensics plays a crucial role in digital investigations, involving the analysis of network traffic and communication protocols to reconstruct the sequence of events leading to a security incident or data breach. Network forensic tools like Wireshark and tcpdump capture and analyze network packets, allowing investigators to identify suspicious network traffic, unauthorized access attempts, and data exfiltration activities. By examining packet headers and payloads, investigators can trace the source and destination of network connections, reconstruct communication sessions, and identify potential indicators of compromise (IOCs) or malicious behavior.

Moreover, mobile device forensics is becoming increasingly important in digital investigations due to the widespread use of smartphones and tablets in both personal and professional settings. Mobile forensics tools like Cellebrite UFED and Oxygen Forensic Detective enable investigators to extract data from mobile devices, including call logs, text messages, photos, videos, and application data, for analysis and examination. By analyzing mobile device artifacts, investigators can uncover evidence of communications, location tracking, and user activities relevant to the investigation.

Additionally, forensic analysis of digital artifacts such as emails, documents, and web browsing history can provide valuable insights into the activities and intentions of individuals involved in a security incident or cybercrime. Forensic tools like EnCase Forensic and Forensic Toolkit (FTK) enable investigators to parse and analyze various types of digital artifacts, including email headers, document metadata, and web browser artifacts, to reconstruct the timeline of events and establish a chain of custody for evidence. Furthermore, digital forensic investigations often involve the use of cryptographic techniques to protect the integrity and confidentiality of digital evidence. Investigators may use cryptographic hashing algorithms such as SHA-256 or MD5 to calculate hash values of files and verify their integrity throughout the investigation process. Similarly, encryption and decryption tools like OpenSSL or GPG are used to encrypt sensitive data during transit or storage, ensuring that only authorized individuals can access and analyze the evidence.

Moreover, forensic reporting and documentation are critical aspects of digital forensic investigations, involving the documentation of findings, analysis, and conclusions in a comprehensive forensic report. Forensic reports provide a detailed account of the investigation process, including the methodology used, evidence collected, analysis performed, and conclusions drawn. Investigators may use tools like Microsoft Word or LaTeX to create forensic reports, ensuring that they are organized, well-documented, and admissible as evidence in legal proceedings.

Additionally, digital forensic investigations often require collaboration and cooperation between various stakeholders, including law enforcement agencies, legal teams, and incident response personnel. Effective communication and coordination among these stakeholders are essential for ensuring the success of the investigation and the timely resolution of security incidents. Collaboration tools like Slack or Microsoft Teams facilitate communication and information sharing among team members, enabling them to collaborate effectively and share updates on the investigation progress.

In summary, digital forensics fundamentals encompass a wide range of techniques, methodologies, and tools used to investigate and analyze digital evidence related to security incidents and cybercrimes. By leveraging forensic analysis techniques such as file system analysis, memory forensics, network forensics, and mobile device forensics, investigators can uncover valuable evidence, reconstruct the sequence of events, and identify perpetrators involved in cyber attacks or data breaches. Moreover, effective documentation, communication, and collaboration are essential for ensuring the success of digital forensic investigations and the prosecution of cybercriminals. Forensic analysis procedures and tools are essential components of digital investigations, enabling forensic analysts to collect, preserve, and analyze digital evidence to uncover the truth behind security incidents and cybercrimes. One of the fundamental procedures in forensic analysis is evidence acquisition, which involves capturing and preserving digital evidence in a forensically sound manner to maintain its integrity and admissibility in court. The foremost tool used for evidence acquisition is the forensic imaging tool, such as FTK Imager or dd command in Unix-like operating systems, which creates a bit-by-bit copy of storage devices, ensuring that the original evidence remains intact for analysis. Once the evidence is acquired, forensic analysts proceed with evidence examination, which involves analyzing the collected data to identify relevant artifacts, such as files, folders, and system configurations, that may provide insights into the incident or crime under investigation. For file analysis, forensic analysts use file analysis tools like Autopsy or The Sleuth Kit, which enable them to examine file metadata, content, and relationships to reconstruct the sequence of events leading to the incident. Additionally, forensic analysts may employ data carving techniques using tools like Scalpel or PhotoRec to recover deleted or fragmented files from storage media, providing additional evidence for the investigation. Moreover, memory analysis is a critical aspect of forensic analysis, allowing analysts to examine the volatile memory (RAM) of a system to identify running processes, network connections, and artifacts related to malicious activities. Memory analysis tools like Volatility Framework or Rekall provide capabilities to extract and analyze memory dumps, enabling analysts to uncover evidence of malware execution, rootkit presence, or unauthorized access to sensitive data stored in memory. Furthermore, network analysis is another important procedure in forensic analysis, involving the examination of network traffic and communication patterns to reconstruct the activities of an attacker or intruder within a network environment. Network analysis tools like Wireshark or tcpdump capture and analyze network packets, allowing analysts to identify suspicious traffic, unauthorized access attempts, and data exfiltration activities that may indicate a security breach or cyber attack. By correlating network traffic with other forensic artifacts, analysts can piece together the sequence of events and identify potential indicators of compromise (IOCs) or malicious behavior.

Additionally, forensic analysis often involves the examination of digital artifacts such as emails, documents, and web browsing history to uncover evidence of communication, intent, or motive related to a security incident or cybercrime. Forensic analysis tools like EnCase Forensic or Forensic Toolkit (FTK) enable analysts to parse and analyze various types of digital artifacts, including email headers, document metadata, and web browser artifacts, to reconstruct the timeline of events and establish a chain of custody for evidence. Moreover, mobile device forensics is becoming increasingly important in forensic analysis, allowing analysts to extract and examine data from smartphones, tablets, and other mobile devices to uncover evidence relevant to an investigation. Mobile device forensics tools like Cellebrite UFED or Oxygen Forensic Detective provide capabilities to extract data from mobile devices, including call logs, text messages, photos, and application data, for analysis and examination.

Furthermore, forensic analysis procedures involve the documentation and reporting of findings, analysis, and conclusions in a comprehensive forensic report. Forensic reports provide a detailed account of the investigation process, including the methodology used, evidence collected, analysis performed, and conclusions drawn. Analysts may use tools like Microsoft Word or LaTeX to create forensic reports, ensuring that they are well-organized, thoroughly documented, and admissible as evidence in legal proceedings. Additionally, collaboration and communication among stakeholders, including law enforcement agencies, legal teams, and incident response personnel, are essential for the success of forensic analysis. Collaboration tools like Slack or Microsoft Teams facilitate communication and information sharing among team members, enabling them to collaborate effectively and share updates on the investigation progress.

In summary, forensic analysis procedures and tools are essential for uncovering digital evidence and reconstructing the sequence of events related to security incidents and cybercrimes. By following established procedures for evidence acquisition, examination, and analysis, forensic analysts can uncover valuable evidence, identify perpetrators, and support legal proceedings against cybercriminals. Moreover, effective documentation, reporting, and collaboration are essential for ensuring the success of forensic analysis and the prosecution of individuals involved in cyber attacks or data breaches.

BOOK 3
RISK MANAGEMENT ESSENTIALS
NAVIGATING SECURITY CHALLENGES IN SY0-701

ROB BOTWRIGHT

Chapter 1: Introduction to Risk Management

Risk management is a critical aspect of any organization's operations, encompassing the processes and strategies used to identify, assess, and mitigate potential risks that may impact its objectives and goals. One fundamental aspect of risk management is risk identification, which involves identifying and documenting potential risks that may arise from internal or external sources within the organization's environment. To effectively identify risks, organizations may conduct risk identification workshops or brainstorming sessions involving key stakeholders to identify a wide range of potential risks across various areas of the organization's operations. Once risks are identified, the next step in the risk management process is risk assessment, which involves evaluating the likelihood and potential impact of each identified risk on the organization's objectives and goals. Risk assessment techniques such as qualitative and quantitative risk analysis help organizations prioritize risks based on their severity and likelihood, allowing them to focus their resources on mitigating the most significant risks first.

Moreover, risk mitigation is a key component of risk management, involving the development and implementation of strategies and controls to reduce the likelihood or impact of identified risks to an acceptable level. Risk mitigation strategies may include risk avoidance, risk transfer, risk reduction, or risk acceptance, depending on the nature and severity of the risk. For example, organizations may choose to avoid certain risks altogether by discontinuing certain activities or entering into contractual agreements to transfer risks to third parties, such as insurance providers. Additionally, organizations may implement risk reduction measures such as implementing security controls, redundancies, or contingency plans to reduce the likelihood or impact of identified risks.

Furthermore, risk monitoring and review are essential aspects of risk management, involving the ongoing monitoring and evaluation of identified risks and the effectiveness of risk mitigation measures implemented by the organization. Risk monitoring ensures that organizations remain vigilant to emerging risks or changes in the risk landscape that may affect their objectives and goals. Regular risk reviews and assessments enable organizations to identify new risks, reassess existing risks, and adjust their risk management strategies and controls accordingly to maintain their effectiveness in mitigating risks. Additionally, risk monitoring and review help organizations ensure compliance with regulatory requirements and industry standards related to risk management practices.

Additionally, risk communication and reporting are vital elements of risk management, involving the communication of risk-related information to key stakeholders within the organization and external parties, such as regulators, shareholders, and customers. Effective risk communication ensures that stakeholders are informed about potential risks facing the organization, the organization's risk management strategies and controls, and the potential impact of risks on the organization's objectives and goals. Clear and transparent risk reporting facilitates informed decision-making by stakeholders and fosters trust and confidence in the organization's ability to manage risks effectively.

Moreover, risk governance is a foundational aspect of risk management, encompassing the structures, processes, and mechanisms used by organizations to oversee and manage risks effectively at all levels of the organization. Risk governance frameworks, such as the Committee of Sponsoring Organizations of the Treadway Commission (COSO) Enterprise Risk Management framework or the ISO 31000 Risk Management framework, provide guidance on establishing risk management policies, roles, responsibilities, and accountability within organizations. Effective risk governance ensures that risk management practices are integrated into the organization's overall governance structure and align with its strategic objectives and values.

Furthermore, risk culture plays a crucial role in risk management, influencing the attitudes, behaviors, and actions of individuals within an organization towards risk-taking and risk management. A positive risk culture fosters open communication, accountability, and proactive risk management practices, enabling organizations to effectively identify, assess, and mitigate risks to achieve their objectives and goals. Organizations can promote a positive risk culture by fostering a supportive and transparent environment that encourages employees to report risks, share knowledge and best practices, and actively participate in risk management initiatives.

In summary, the fundamentals of risk management encompass a holistic approach to identifying, assessing, and mitigating risks that may impact an organization's objectives and goals. By implementing robust risk management processes and controls, organizations can effectively navigate uncertainties and challenges, protect their assets and reputation, and seize opportunities for growth and innovation. Moreover, cultivating a positive risk culture and fostering effective risk governance structures are essential for embedding risk management practices into the organization's DNA and ensuring its long-term success and sustainability.

Risk management is a cornerstone of security practices, serving as a linchpin in safeguarding assets, maintaining continuity, and ensuring organizational resilience in the face of ever-evolving threats and vulnerabilities. It serves as a proactive approach to addressing potential risks that may compromise the confidentiality, integrity, and availability of critical assets and information systems within an organization. By systematically identifying, assessing, and mitigating risks, organizations can effectively allocate resources, prioritize security initiatives, and optimize their security posture to align with their business objectives and risk tolerance levels.

One of the primary reasons for the importance of risk management in security is its role in helping organizations anticipate and prepare for potential security incidents and breaches, thereby reducing the likelihood of their occurrence and minimizing their impact when they do occur. Through risk assessments and threat modeling exercises, organizations can identify potential vulnerabilities, threats, and attack vectors that may exploit weaknesses in their security defenses, allowing them to proactively implement controls and countermeasures to mitigate these risks before they manifest into security incidents.

Moreover, risk management provides organizations with a structured framework for making informed decisions about security investments, resource allocations, and risk mitigation strategies based on a thorough understanding of the risks facing the organization and their potential impact on business operations. By quantifying and prioritizing risks, organizations can effectively allocate resources to address the most critical risks first, thereby optimizing the effectiveness of their security investments and maximizing the return on investment (ROI) in security initiatives.

Furthermore, risk management fosters a culture of accountability, transparency, and continuous improvement within organizations by encouraging stakeholders at all levels to actively participate in the risk management process and take ownership of security risks within their respective areas of responsibility. By promoting cross-functional collaboration and communication, risk management helps break down silos and create a shared understanding of security risks across the organization, enabling stakeholders to work together towards common security objectives and goals.

Additionally, risk management plays a crucial role in regulatory compliance and governance by helping organizations identify and address security risks that may impact their compliance with applicable laws, regulations, and industry standards. By implementing robust risk management practices, organizations can demonstrate due diligence and regulatory compliance to regulatory authorities, auditors, and other stakeholders, thereby avoiding potential legal liabilities, penalties, and reputational damage associated with non-compliance.

Furthermore, risk management enables organizations to adapt and respond effectively to emerging threats and changes in the threat landscape by providing a flexible and adaptive approach to security that can evolve with evolving business needs and security requirements. By continuously monitoring and reassessing risks, organizations can identify new threats, vulnerabilities, and emerging attack vectors and adjust their security strategies and controls accordingly to mitigate these risks effectively.

Moreover, risk management helps organizations build resilience and enhance their ability to recover from security incidents and breaches by developing and implementing robust incident response and business continuity plans that enable them to respond promptly and effectively to security incidents, minimize their impact on business operations, and restore normal operations in a timely manner. By integrating risk management with incident response and business continuity planning, organizations can ensure a coordinated and holistic approach to managing security risks and mitigating their impact on business operations. In summary, the importance of risk management in security cannot be overstated, as it serves as a foundational pillar of effective security practices, enabling organizations to anticipate, assess, and mitigate security risks proactively, allocate resources efficiently, and enhance their resilience to security threats and vulnerabilities. By embedding risk management into their organizational culture and governance structures, organizations can foster a proactive and adaptive approach to security that enables them to address evolving threats and safeguard their assets, reputation, and business continuity effectively.

Chapter 2: Understanding Risk Assessment Methodologies

Risk assessment processes are fundamental components of any effective risk management strategy, providing organizations with the means to identify, analyze, and prioritize potential risks that may impact their objectives and operations. These processes involve systematic evaluations of various factors, including threats, vulnerabilities, and the potential consequences of risks, to inform decision-making and risk mitigation efforts. One commonly used method for conducting risk assessments is the "qualitative risk assessment," which involves evaluating risks based on their likelihood and potential impact using subjective judgments rather than precise numerical measurements. Another approach is the "quantitative risk assessment," which involves assigning numerical values to risks based on factors such as probability and magnitude of impact to calculate the overall risk exposure. These assessments provide organizations with valuable insights into the risks they face and enable them to make informed decisions about resource allocation and risk mitigation strategies.

Moreover, risk assessment processes typically involve several key steps, beginning with the identification of risks through techniques such as risk brainstorming sessions, interviews, and document reviews to compile a comprehensive list of potential risks facing the organization. Once risks are identified, they are typically analyzed to assess their likelihood and potential impact on the organization's objectives and operations. This analysis may involve the use of risk assessment matrices or scoring systems to assign numerical values to risks based on predetermined criteria, such as severity, likelihood, and detectability.

Furthermore, after risks are analyzed, organizations typically prioritize them based on their severity and likelihood using risk prioritization techniques such as risk ranking or risk scoring to focus resources on addressing the most critical risks first. This prioritization enables organizations to allocate resources effectively and implement risk mitigation strategies that target the most significant risks to minimize their potential impact on the organization.

Additionally, risk assessment processes often involve the development and implementation of risk mitigation plans to address identified risks and reduce their likelihood or impact on the organization. These plans may include strategies such as risk avoidance, risk reduction, risk transfer, or risk acceptance, depending on the nature and severity of the risks identified. For example, organizations may choose to avoid certain risks altogether by discontinuing certain activities or entering into contractual agreements to transfer risks to third parties, such as insurance providers.

Moreover, risk assessment processes are iterative and ongoing, requiring organizations to regularly review and reassess risks to ensure that their risk management strategies remain effective in addressing evolving threats and changing business conditions. Regular risk assessments enable organizations to identify new risks, reassess existing risks, and adjust their risk management strategies and controls accordingly to maintain their effectiveness in mitigating risks.

Furthermore, effective risk assessment processes require the involvement and collaboration of key stakeholders across the organization, including executives, managers, employees, and external partners, to ensure that a comprehensive and holistic approach to risk management is adopted. By engaging stakeholders from different functional areas and levels of the organization, organizations can leverage diverse perspectives and expertise to identify and assess risks more effectively and develop risk mitigation strategies that are aligned with organizational objectives and priorities.

In summary, risk assessment processes are essential components of effective risk management practices, providing organizations with the means to identify, analyze, and prioritize potential risks that may impact their objectives and operations. By systematically evaluating risks and developing risk mitigation strategies, organizations can enhance their resilience to threats, protect their assets and reputation, and achieve their business objectives in a dynamic and uncertain environment.

Comparative analysis of risk assessment models is crucial for organizations seeking to implement effective risk management strategies tailored to their specific needs and circumstances. Various risk assessment models exist, each with its own strengths, weaknesses, and suitability for different organizational contexts. One widely used model is the NIST Risk Management Framework (RMF), which provides a structured and systematic approach to managing risks associated with information security. The NIST RMF consists of six steps: prepare, categorize, select, implement, assess, and authorize. Another popular model is the ISO 27001 risk assessment process, which is based on the Plan-Do-Check-Act (PDCA) cycle and involves identifying assets, assessing risks, and implementing controls to mitigate those risks. Additionally, the OCTAVE (Operationally Critical Threat, Asset, and Vulnerability Evaluation) model is a risk assessment methodology developed by the CERT Coordination Center that focuses on identifying and mitigating risks to critical assets and operations within an organization. Each of these models has its own set of advantages and limitations, and organizations must carefully evaluate their requirements and objectives to determine which model is most suitable for their needs.

Furthermore, one of the key factors to consider when comparing risk assessment models is their level of complexity and resource requirements. Some models, such as the NIST RMF, may be more comprehensive and suitable for large organizations with dedicated risk management teams and resources, while others, such as the OCTAVE model, may be more streamlined and suitable for smaller organizations with limited resources and expertise. Additionally, organizations must consider the scalability of the risk assessment model and its ability to accommodate changes in the organization's risk landscape over time.

Moreover, another important consideration when comparing risk assessment models is their alignment with industry standards and best practices. Models that are based on widely accepted standards, such as the ISO 27001 risk assessment process, may offer greater credibility and assurance that the organization's risk management practices are in line with industry norms and expectations. Additionally, organizations may also consider the availability of supporting tools and resources, such as software applications or guidance documentation, to facilitate the implementation of the risk assessment model and ensure its effectiveness.

Additionally, organizations must evaluate the flexibility and adaptability of risk assessment models to accommodate their unique business requirements and risk profiles. Some models may offer greater flexibility in terms of customization and tailoring to specific organizational needs, while others may be more rigid and prescriptive in their approach. Moreover, organizations must consider the comprehensiveness and coverage of the risk assessment model in addressing a wide range of risks and vulnerabilities across different areas of the organization, including information technology, physical security, personnel, and operations.

Furthermore, organizations must consider the level of expertise and training required to implement and maintain the chosen risk assessment model effectively.

Some models may require specialized knowledge and skills in risk management principles, methodologies, and techniques, while others may be more straightforward and accessible to non-specialists. Additionally, organizations must consider the cost implications of implementing and maintaining the chosen risk assessment model, including any upfront investments in training, tools, or consulting services, as well as ongoing operational costs.

In summary, comparative analysis of risk assessment models is essential for organizations seeking to establish effective risk management practices that align with their objectives, resources, and risk profiles. By carefully evaluating the advantages, limitations, and suitability of different models, organizations can make informed decisions about which model best meets their needs and enables them to identify, assess, and mitigate risks effectively. Moreover, by considering factors such as complexity, alignment with industry standards, flexibility, and resource requirements, organizations can ensure that their chosen risk assessment model is well-suited to their unique circumstances and contributes to the overall success of their risk management efforts.

Chapter 3: Risk Mitigation Strategies

Risk mitigation planning and implementation are critical components of an organization's risk management strategy, aimed at reducing the impact and likelihood of potential risks on its objectives and operations. The process involves identifying, assessing, and prioritizing risks and then developing and executing strategies to minimize their adverse effects. One common approach to risk mitigation is to implement controls or measures that reduce the likelihood of risks occurring or their impact if they do occur. For example, organizations can deploy firewalls to protect their networks from unauthorized access or intrusion detection systems (IDS) to monitor for suspicious activity. These measures help to strengthen the organization's defenses against potential threats and vulnerabilities. Additionally, organizations can implement policies and procedures to govern employee behavior and enforce compliance with security best practices, such as regular password changes or data encryption. By establishing clear guidelines and expectations, organizations can reduce the risk of security breaches and ensure that employees understand their roles and responsibilities in maintaining a secure environment.

Moreover, another effective risk mitigation strategy is to transfer risk to third parties through insurance or contractual agreements. For example, organizations can purchase cyber insurance policies to protect against financial losses resulting from data breaches or other security incidents. Similarly, organizations can outsource certain functions or services to third-party vendors who specialize in security, such as managed security service providers (MSSPs) or cloud service providers (CSPs). By transferring risk to external partners with greater expertise and resources, organizations can reduce their exposure to potential threats and vulnerabilities.

Furthermore, organizations can also accept certain risks if the cost of mitigation outweighs the potential impact of the risk. This approach involves conducting a cost-benefit analysis to determine whether investing resources in mitigating a particular risk is justified based on its likelihood and potential impact. For example, organizations may choose to accept the risk of a minor security vulnerability if the cost of patching it outweighs the potential impact of a security breach. However, it is essential for organizations to carefully evaluate the potential consequences of accepting risks and ensure that they have appropriate contingency plans in place to mitigate any adverse effects.

Additionally, risk mitigation planning and implementation require ongoing monitoring and evaluation to ensure that the chosen strategies are effective in reducing risks to an acceptable level. This involves regularly assessing the effectiveness of controls and measures, monitoring for changes in the risk landscape, and adjusting mitigation strategies as needed. For example, organizations can conduct regular security assessments or penetration tests to identify weaknesses in their defenses and address them proactively. Likewise, organizations can monitor security logs and alerts generated by security tools to detect and respond to potential security incidents in real-time.

Moreover, effective risk mitigation planning and implementation require the involvement and collaboration of key stakeholders across the organization, including executives, managers, employees, and external partners. By engaging stakeholders from different functional areas and levels of the organization, organizations can leverage diverse perspectives and expertise to identify risks and develop appropriate mitigation strategies. Additionally, communication and coordination are essential for ensuring that mitigation efforts are aligned with organizational objectives and priorities and that resources are allocated effectively.

Furthermore, organizations can leverage risk management frameworks and standards, such as the NIST Risk Management Framework (RMF) or the ISO 31000 Risk Management Standard, to guide their risk mitigation efforts. These frameworks provide structured approaches to identifying, assessing, and mitigating risks and can help organizations establish robust risk management processes and practices. By following established frameworks and standards, organizations can ensure that their risk mitigation efforts are comprehensive, systematic, and aligned with industry best practices.

In summary, risk mitigation planning and implementation are essential components of effective risk management practices, enabling organizations to reduce the impact and likelihood of potential risks on their objectives and operations. By implementing controls, transferring risk, accepting certain risks, and monitoring and evaluating mitigation efforts, organizations can strengthen their defenses against threats and vulnerabilities and enhance their resilience to security incidents. Moreover, by engaging stakeholders, leveraging risk management frameworks, and following industry best practices, organizations can establish robust risk mitigation processes that contribute to their overall success and sustainability.

Proactive risk reduction techniques play a crucial role in mitigating potential threats and vulnerabilities before they escalate into significant security incidents. These techniques involve identifying and addressing risks proactively rather than waiting for them to materialize. One common proactive risk reduction technique is regular vulnerability scanning, which involves using tools such as Nessus or OpenVAS to scan IT systems and networks for known vulnerabilities. These tools identify security weaknesses that could be exploited by attackers and enable organizations to patch or mitigate them before they are exploited. Additionally, organizations can conduct penetration testing, also known as ethical hacking, to identify and address potential security vulnerabilities before attackers do. Penetration testing involves simulating real-world attacks on IT systems and networks to identify weaknesses in defenses and validate the effectiveness of security controls.

Moreover, another proactive risk reduction technique is security awareness training for employees, which helps to educate them about security best practices and how to recognize and respond to security threats. Training programs can cover topics such as phishing awareness, password hygiene, and social engineering tactics, empowering employees to play an active role in protecting organizational assets. Additionally, organizations can implement security policies and procedures that promote a culture of security and establish clear guidelines for acceptable behavior. By setting expectations and providing guidance, organizations can reduce the likelihood of security incidents caused by human error or negligence.

Furthermore, proactive risk reduction techniques also involve implementing security controls and measures that strengthen defenses against potential threats. For example, organizations can deploy firewalls, intrusion detection systems (IDS), and antivirus software to protect their networks and endpoints from unauthorized access and malicious activity. These tools help to monitor and filter network traffic, detect suspicious behavior, and block or quarantine threats in real-time. Additionally, organizations can implement multi-factor authentication (MFA) to add an extra layer of security to user accounts and prevent unauthorized access. MFA requires users to provide multiple forms of identification, such as a password and a one-time code sent to their mobile device, before granting access to sensitive resources.

Moreover, proactive risk reduction techniques involve staying informed about emerging threats and vulnerabilities and taking proactive steps to address them. Organizations can subscribe to threat intelligence feeds from reputable sources, such as the Department of Homeland Security (DHS) or the Cybersecurity and Infrastructure Security Agency (CISA), to receive timely updates about new threats and vulnerabilities. Additionally, organizations can participate in information-sharing forums and industry groups to exchange threat intelligence and collaborate with peers on security best practices. By staying ahead of emerging threats, organizations can take proactive measures to protect their assets and mitigate potential risks.

Additionally, proactive risk reduction techniques include implementing security controls and measures that align with industry standards and best practices. For example, organizations can adopt the CIS Controls, a set of prioritized cybersecurity best practices developed by the Center for Internet Security (CIS), to establish a baseline of security measures that address common threats and vulnerabilities. Similarly, organizations can follow the recommendations outlined in the NIST Cybersecurity Framework (CSF) to identify, protect, detect, respond to, and recover from cybersecurity risks. By adhering to established standards and frameworks, organizations can ensure that their security controls and measures are comprehensive, effective, and aligned with industry norms and expectations.

Furthermore, proactive risk reduction techniques involve conducting risk assessments and developing risk management plans that prioritize and address the most significant risks to the organization. Risk assessments help organizations identify and analyze potential threats and vulnerabilities, assess their potential impact and likelihood, and prioritize them based on their severity. Organizations can then develop risk management plans that outline strategies for mitigating and monitoring these risks, assigning responsibilities, and allocating resources accordingly. By taking a proactive approach to risk management, organizations can identify and address potential threats and vulnerabilities before they pose a significant risk to their operations and reputation.

In summary, proactive risk reduction techniques are essential for organizations seeking to mitigate potential threats and vulnerabilities before they escalate into significant security incidents. By conducting vulnerability scanning, penetration testing, security awareness training, and implementing security controls and measures aligned with industry standards and best practices, organizations can strengthen their defenses and enhance their resilience to cyber threats. Additionally, by staying informed about emerging threats and vulnerabilities and conducting regular risk assessments, organizations can identify and address potential risks proactively, reducing the likelihood and impact of security incidents on their operations and stakeholders.

Chapter 4: Quantitative Risk Analysis Techniques

Quantifying risk exposure is a critical aspect of risk management, enabling organizations to assess the potential impact of identified risks on their objectives and operations. One commonly used method for quantifying risk exposure is the Annualized Loss Expectancy (ALE) calculation, which helps organizations estimate the financial impact of a potential risk over a one-year period. The ALE calculation involves multiplying the Annual Rate of Occurrence (ARO) by the Single Loss Expectancy (SLE). The ARO represents the expected frequency of a particular risk occurring within a year, while the SLE represents the financial loss associated with a single occurrence of that risk. For example, if a security breach occurs on average once every five years (ARO = 0.2) and the estimated financial loss resulting from the breach is $100,000 (SLE = $100,000), the ALE would be $20,000 ($100,000 * 0.2). By quantifying risk exposure using the ALE calculation, organizations can prioritize their risk mitigation efforts and allocate resources effectively based on the potential impact of identified risks.

Furthermore, another method for quantifying risk exposure is the Risk Priority Number (RPN) calculation, which is commonly used in risk assessment and management processes such as Failure Mode and Effects Analysis (FMEA) and Hazard Analysis and Critical Control Points (HACCP). The RPN calculation involves multiplying the severity, occurrence, and detection ratings assigned to a particular risk to determine its overall priority. The severity rating represents the potential impact of the risk on organizational objectives or operations, the occurrence rating represents the likelihood of the risk occurring, and the detection rating represents the organization's ability to detect and respond to the risk before it materializes. By quantifying risk exposure using the RPN calculation, organizations can prioritize their risk mitigation efforts and focus on addressing high-priority risks that pose the greatest threat to their operations.

Moreover, organizations can use qualitative risk assessment techniques, such as risk matrices or risk heat maps, to assess and categorize risks based on their potential impact and likelihood. These techniques involve assigning scores or rankings to risks based on predefined criteria, such as severity, likelihood, or impact, and mapping them onto a matrix or heat map to visualize their relative importance. By categorizing risks qualitatively, organizations can gain insights into the overall risk landscape and identify areas of vulnerability or concern that require further attention. Additionally, qualitative risk assessment techniques can help organizations communicate risk information effectively to stakeholders and facilitate informed decision-making about risk management priorities and strategies.

Additionally, organizations can use quantitative risk assessment techniques, such as Monte Carlo simulation or sensitivity analysis, to model and analyze the potential impact of identified risks on organizational objectives or operations. Monte Carlo simulation involves running multiple simulations of a risk scenario using probabilistic models and input variables to estimate the range of possible outcomes and their associated probabilities. Sensitivity analysis involves assessing the sensitivity of risk outcomes to changes in input variables or assumptions to identify key drivers of risk exposure and inform decision-making about risk mitigation strategies. By using quantitative risk assessment techniques, organizations can gain a more nuanced understanding of the potential impact of identified risks and make more informed decisions about risk management priorities and resource allocation.

Furthermore, organizations can use risk aggregation and correlation techniques to assess the cumulative impact of multiple risks on organizational objectives or operations. Risk aggregation involves combining individual risk assessments into a comprehensive view of overall risk exposure, taking into account dependencies and interactions between different risks. Risk correlation involves analyzing the degree of correlation or dependence between individual risks to understand how changes in one risk may affect others. By aggregating and correlating risks, organizations can identify potential synergies or cascading effects that may amplify or mitigate overall risk exposure and inform decision-making about risk management strategies.

Moreover, organizations can use risk tolerance and appetite metrics to establish thresholds or limits for acceptable levels of risk exposure based on their organizational objectives, values, and stakeholders' expectations. Risk tolerance represents the maximum acceptable level of risk exposure that an organization is willing to accept to achieve its objectives, while risk appetite represents the organization's willingness to take on risk in pursuit of opportunities or strategic objectives. By defining clear risk tolerance and appetite metrics, organizations can align their risk management activities with their strategic goals and ensure that risk-taking decisions are consistent with their overall risk management philosophy and objectives.

Additionally, organizations can use Key Risk Indicators (KRIs) and Key Performance Indicators (KPIs) to monitor and track changes in risk exposure over time and evaluate the effectiveness of risk management strategies. KRIs are leading indicators that provide early warning signs of potential risks or vulnerabilities, while KPIs are lagging indicators that measure the performance or effectiveness of risk management activities. By monitoring KRIs and KPIs, organizations can identify emerging risks, assess the impact of risk management efforts, and make data-driven decisions about adjusting risk management strategies or allocating resources to address evolving threats and vulnerabilities.

In summary, quantifying risk exposure is essential for organizations seeking to understand and manage the potential impact of identified risks on their objectives and operations. By using a combination of quantitative and qualitative risk assessment techniques, organizations can gain insights into the likelihood and severity of risks, prioritize their risk management efforts, and make informed decisions about resource allocation and risk mitigation strategies. Additionally, by establishing clear risk tolerance and appetite metrics, monitoring KRIs and KPIs, and leveraging risk aggregation and correlation techniques, organizations can develop robust risk management processes that align with their strategic goals and objectives and enable them to navigate uncertainty and complexity effectively.

Risk metrics and measurement methods play a pivotal role in the comprehensive assessment and management of risks within an organization's operational landscape, providing valuable insights into the severity, likelihood, and potential impact of identified risks. One widely used risk metric is the Risk Exposure Factor (REF), which quantifies the potential financial loss associated with a specific risk event. The REF is calculated by multiplying the Single Loss Expectancy (SLE) by the Annualized Rate of Occurrence (ARO), providing organizations with a quantitative assessment of the potential financial impact of a particular risk over a given time frame. For instance, if the SLE of a data breach is $100,000 and the ARO is 0.05 (indicating an average of five breaches per year), the REF would be $5,000 ($100,000 * 0.05), highlighting the potential annual financial loss attributable to the risk. Another essential risk metric is the Risk Priority Number (RPN), which evaluates the severity, occurrence, and detection ratings of a risk to determine its overall priority for mitigation efforts. The RPN is calculated by multiplying the severity, occurrence, and detection ratings assigned to a risk, enabling organizations to prioritize their risk management activities based on the relative importance and potential impact of identified risks. By assigning numerical values to these key risk attributes and combining them into a single metric, organizations can streamline their risk assessment processes and focus their resources on addressing high-priority risks that pose the greatest threat to their objectives and operations.

Moreover, organizations often utilize Key Risk Indicators (KRIs) as a proactive monitoring tool to assess the likelihood and severity of emerging risks and vulnerabilities. KRIs are leading indicators that provide early warning signs of potential risk events, enabling organizations to take preemptive action to mitigate their impact. For example, in the context of cybersecurity, KRIs may include metrics such as the number of detected security incidents, the volume of failed login attempts, or the frequency of malware infections. By monitoring these key indicators in real-time, organizations can identify trends and patterns indicative of heightened risk exposure and implement targeted interventions to prevent or minimize potential harm. Additionally, organizations may employ Key Performance Indicators (KPIs) to measure the effectiveness of their risk management processes and controls. KPIs are lagging indicators that quantify the performance of risk management activities and outcomes, providing organizations with valuable insights into the efficacy of their risk mitigation strategies. Examples of risk management KPIs may include metrics such as the percentage reduction in security incidents, the time taken to detect and respond to security breaches, or the cost savings achieved through proactive risk mitigation efforts. By tracking these performance metrics over time, organizations can assess their progress towards achieving their risk management objectives and identify areas for improvement or refinement.

Furthermore, organizations may utilize qualitative risk measurement methods, such as risk matrices or risk heat maps, to assess and visualize the relative importance and severity of identified risks. These techniques involve categorizing risks based on their potential impact and likelihood and mapping them onto a matrix or heat map to provide a graphical representation of the risk landscape. By visually depicting the distribution of risks according to their severity and likelihood, organizations can gain a holistic understanding of their risk profile and identify areas of concentration or concern that warrant further attention. Additionally, qualitative risk measurement methods can facilitate communication and decision-making by providing stakeholders with a clear and intuitive representation of the organization's risk exposure and priorities. Moreover, organizations may leverage benchmarking and industry standards to compare their risk management performance against peers and best practices. Benchmarking involves measuring and evaluating an organization's risk management practices and outcomes against those of comparable organizations or industry standards, enabling organizations to identify areas of strength and weakness and implement targeted improvements. By benchmarking their risk management performance against industry leaders and recognized standards, organizations can gain valuable insights into emerging trends and best practices and enhance their overall risk management capabilities.

In summary, risk metrics and measurement methods are essential tools for assessing, prioritizing, and managing risks within an organization's operational environment. By quantifying and visualizing risks using metrics such as REF and RPN, organizations can prioritize their risk management efforts and allocate resources effectively to address high-priority risks. Additionally, by monitoring KRIs and KPIs, organizations can proactively identify and respond to emerging risks and vulnerabilities, minimizing their potential impact on organizational objectives and operations. Qualitative risk measurement methods, such as risk matrices and heat maps, provide organizations with a visual representation of their risk landscape, facilitating communication and decision-making. Furthermore, benchmarking and industry standards enable organizations to assess their risk management performance against peers and best practices, driving continuous improvement and innovation in risk management practices. By leveraging these tools and techniques, organizations can build resilience and adaptability in the face of evolving threats and uncertainties, ensuring their long-term success and sustainability.

Chapter 5: Qualitative Risk Evaluation Approaches

Qualitative risk assessment methods serve as fundamental tools in evaluating risks within an organization's operational landscape, providing valuable insights into the nature, severity, and potential impact of identified risks. One widely used qualitative risk assessment method is the Risk Matrix, which involves categorizing risks based on their likelihood and consequence scores to determine their overall risk rating. The Risk Matrix typically consists of a grid with likelihood and consequence axes, with risks plotted according to their assessed likelihood and consequence levels. By mapping risks onto the matrix, organizations can visually identify high-priority risks that require immediate attention and mitigation efforts. Another common qualitative risk assessment method is the Risk Heat Map, which provides a graphical representation of risks based on their likelihood and impact. Risks are color-coded or shaded on the heat map according to their assessed likelihood and impact levels, allowing organizations to quickly identify areas of high risk and focus their risk management efforts accordingly.

Additionally, organizations may utilize Risk Registers to document and track identified risks throughout the risk management process. A Risk Register is a comprehensive database or spreadsheet that contains detailed information about each identified risk, including its description, likelihood, consequence, mitigation measures, and assigned risk owner. By maintaining a centralized repository of risks, organizations can systematically manage and monitor their risk exposure, track the status of mitigation activities, and facilitate communication and collaboration among stakeholders. Moreover, organizations may conduct Risk Workshops or brainstorming sessions to engage key stakeholders in the qualitative risk assessment process. These collaborative sessions bring together individuals with diverse perspectives and expertise to identify, assess, and prioritize risks based on their collective knowledge and experience. By fostering open dialogue and collaboration, Risk Workshops enable organizations to gain a comprehensive understanding of their risk landscape and develop effective risk management strategies.

Furthermore, organizations may employ Scenario Analysis as a qualitative risk assessment technique to evaluate the potential impact of different risk scenarios on their operations and objectives. Scenario Analysis involves creating hypothetical scenarios or "what-if" situations to explore the possible outcomes and consequences of specific risks. By simulating different scenarios and assessing their potential impact, organizations can identify vulnerabilities, gaps, and dependencies within their systems and processes and develop contingency plans to mitigate potential risks. Additionally, organizations may utilize Delphi Technique to gather expert opinions and insights on identified risks and their potential impact. The Delphi Technique involves soliciting input from a panel of subject matter experts through a series of structured questionnaires or surveys. Experts anonymously provide their assessments and opinions on identified risks, which are then aggregated and analyzed to reach a consensus on the likelihood, consequence, and significance of each risk.

Moreover, organizations may conduct SWOT Analysis as a qualitative risk assessment method to identify and evaluate their strengths, weaknesses, opportunities, and threats. SWOT Analysis involves examining internal strengths and weaknesses, such as organizational capabilities and resources, as well as external opportunities and threats, such as market trends and competitive pressures. By analyzing these factors in relation to identified risks, organizations can develop strategies to capitalize on strengths, mitigate weaknesses, seize opportunities, and mitigate threats effectively. Additionally, organizations may employ Bowtie Analysis as a qualitative risk assessment technique to visually map the causes, consequences, and controls associated with specific risks. Bowtie Analysis involves creating a diagram that illustrates the relationship between potential risk events (the "top event"), their causes (the "left-hand side"), and their consequences (the "right-hand side"). By identifying critical control measures and barriers to prevent or mitigate the occurrence of the top event, organizations can enhance their risk management capabilities and resilience.

In summary, qualitative risk assessment methods are essential tools for organizations to evaluate and manage risks effectively within their operational environment. By employing techniques such as Risk Matrix, Risk Heat Map, Risk Registers, and Scenario Analysis, organizations can identify, assess, and prioritize risks based on their likelihood, consequence, and potential impact. Additionally, collaborative approaches such as Risk Workshops and Delphi Technique enable organizations to leverage the collective expertise and insights of key stakeholders in the risk assessment process. Furthermore, SWOT Analysis and Bowtie Analysis provide organizations with valuable frameworks for identifying internal and external factors that may influence their risk exposure and developing targeted risk management strategies. By incorporating these qualitative risk assessment methods into their risk management practices, organizations can enhance their ability to anticipate, mitigate, and respond to emerging risks and uncertainties effectively.

Risk ranking and prioritization techniques are crucial components of effective risk management strategies, enabling organizations to identify and address their most significant risks systematically. One commonly used technique is the Risk Priority Number (RPN), which assesses risks based on their likelihood, severity, and detectability scores. The RPN is calculated by multiplying the likelihood, severity, and detectability scores assigned to each risk, resulting in a numerical value that represents its overall priority. Organizations can then prioritize risks based on their RPN values, focusing their resources and efforts on mitigating high-priority risks with the highest RPN scores first. Another widely used technique is the Risk Scoring Matrix, which categorizes risks into predefined risk levels based on their likelihood and impact scores. The Risk Scoring Matrix typically consists of a grid with likelihood and impact axes, with risks classified into risk levels such as low, medium, and high based on their assessed likelihood and impact levels. By mapping risks onto the matrix and assigning them to appropriate risk levels, organizations can prioritize risks according to their severity and allocate resources accordingly.

Additionally, organizations may employ the Risk-Based Approach, which involves prioritizing risks based on their potential impact on organizational objectives and goals. The Risk-Based Approach considers factors such as the organization's mission, vision, strategic objectives, and stakeholder expectations when assessing and prioritizing risks. By aligning risk management activities with organizational priorities and strategic objectives, organizations can focus on mitigating risks that pose the greatest threat to achieving their desired outcomes. Furthermore, organizations may utilize the Pareto Principle, also known as the 80/20 rule, to prioritize risks effectively. The Pareto Principle suggests that approximately 80% of the effects come from 20% of the causes, implying that a small number of risks are likely to account for a significant portion of the overall risk exposure. By identifying and addressing the most critical risks that contribute to the majority of the risk exposure, organizations can maximize the impact of their risk management efforts and resources.

Moreover, organizations may employ Risk Triage as a prioritization technique to assess and categorize risks based on their urgency and importance. Risk Triage involves evaluating risks based on criteria such as the likelihood and severity of their potential consequences, as well as their proximity to key milestones or deadlines. Risks are then categorized into priority levels such as high, medium, and low, with high-priority risks requiring immediate attention and mitigation efforts. Additionally, organizations may utilize Cost-Benefit Analysis to prioritize risks by comparing the expected costs of risk mitigation measures to the potential benefits or savings they would yield. By evaluating the costs and benefits of different risk mitigation options, organizations can make informed decisions about resource allocation and prioritize risk management activities accordingly.

Furthermore, organizations may utilize Risk Appetite and Risk Tolerance as guiding principles for risk prioritization. Risk appetite refers to the level of risk that an organization is willing to accept or tolerate in pursuit of its objectives, while risk tolerance represents the acceptable variation or deviation from desired outcomes. By establishing clear risk appetite and tolerance thresholds, organizations can prioritize risks that fall within acceptable limits and focus their attention on mitigating risks that exceed these thresholds. Additionally, organizations may employ

Multi-Criteria Decision Analysis (MCDA) as a structured approach to prioritize risks based on multiple criteria or factors. MCDA involves evaluating risks against predefined criteria such as likelihood, severity, cost, and strategic importance and assigning weights to each criterion based on its relative importance. By aggregating scores across multiple criteria, organizations can rank risks objectively and make informed decisions about risk prioritization and mitigation.

In summary, risk ranking and prioritization techniques play a vital role in helping organizations identify, assess, and address their most significant risks effectively. By employing techniques such as the Risk Priority Number, Risk Scoring Matrix, Risk-Based Approach, Pareto Principle, Risk Triage, Cost-Benefit Analysis, Risk Appetite, Risk Tolerance, and Multi-Criteria Decision Analysis, organizations can prioritize risks based on their likelihood, severity, impact on organizational objectives, urgency, and cost-effectiveness of mitigation measures. By focusing their resources and efforts on mitigating high-priority risks that pose the greatest threat to achieving organizational goals, organizations can enhance their resilience, protect their assets, and sustain long-term success in an increasingly complex and dynamic risk environment.

Chapter 6: Implementing Risk Controls

Risk control selection and implementation are critical aspects of the risk management process, enabling organizations to mitigate identified risks and reduce their potential impact on business operations. One commonly used approach for selecting and implementing risk controls is the NIST Risk Management Framework (RMF), which provides a structured and systematic methodology for managing organizational risks. The NIST RMF consists of six steps: prepare, categorize, select, implement, assess, and authorize. During the prepare phase, organizations establish the context for risk management activities by defining their risk management strategy, objectives, and scope. They also identify key stakeholders and allocate resources for risk management activities. In the categorize phase, organizations classify information systems and assets based on their impact levels and define the risk tolerance for each system or asset. This classification helps prioritize risk management efforts and ensures that resources are allocated effectively.

Once assets and systems are categorized, organizations move to the select phase, where they identify and prioritize risk controls based on their effectiveness in mitigating identified risks. This phase involves evaluating available risk control options and selecting controls that are appropriate for addressing specific risks. Organizations may use various criteria, such as cost-effectiveness, feasibility, and alignment with organizational objectives, to prioritize risk controls. For example, in a network security context, organizations may choose to implement firewalls, intrusion detection systems (IDS), and access control mechanisms to mitigate network-related risks.

After selecting risk controls, organizations proceed to the implement phase, where they deploy the selected controls and integrate them into their existing processes and systems. This phase involves configuring, installing, and testing the effectiveness of the chosen controls to ensure they adequately address identified risks. For instance, organizations may configure firewalls to filter incoming and outgoing network traffic, restrict access to sensitive resources, and block known malicious IP addresses using command-line interface (CLI) commands such as iptables in Linux or netsh advfirewall in Windows.

Following the implementation of risk controls, organizations enter the assess phase, where they evaluate the effectiveness of deployed controls in mitigating identified risks. This phase involves conducting regular assessments and audits to verify that risk controls are functioning as intended and providing the desired level of protection. Organizations may use tools such as vulnerability scanners, penetration testing frameworks, and security information and event management (SIEM) solutions to assess the effectiveness of deployed controls and identify any gaps or vulnerabilities.

Once risk controls have been assessed and validated, organizations move to the authorize phase, where they formally accept the residual risks associated with their systems and assets. This phase involves obtaining approval from relevant stakeholders, such as senior management or regulatory authorities, to operate the systems and assets under the defined risk conditions. Organizations may document their risk acceptance decisions and develop risk acceptance criteria to ensure that residual risks remain within acceptable limits.

In addition to the NIST RMF, organizations may leverage other frameworks and standards, such as ISO 27001, COBIT, and COSO, to guide their risk control selection and implementation efforts. These frameworks provide best practices, guidelines, and controls for managing various aspects of organizational risk, including information security, compliance, and governance. By aligning with recognized frameworks and standards, organizations can ensure that their risk management practices are comprehensive, consistent, and aligned with industry best practices.

Furthermore, organizations should adopt a continuous improvement approach to risk control selection and implementation, regularly reviewing and updating their risk management processes and controls in response to changes in the threat landscape, business environment, and regulatory requirements. This iterative approach allows organizations to adapt to evolving risks and emerging threats effectively. By continuously monitoring, assessing, and enhancing their risk controls, organizations can strengthen their resilience, minimize potential losses, and protect their assets and reputation in an increasingly complex and dynamic risk landscape.

Monitoring and reviewing the effectiveness of risk controls is essential for maintaining the security posture of an organization over time. This process involves regularly assessing whether implemented controls are functioning as intended and providing adequate protection against identified risks. One commonly used method for monitoring risk controls effectiveness is through the use of security metrics and key performance indicators (KPIs). These metrics allow organizations to quantitatively measure the performance of their risk controls and track changes in risk levels over time. For example, organizations may measure the number of security incidents detected by their intrusion detection systems (IDS) or the time taken to remediate identified vulnerabilities in their systems using vulnerability management tools.

In addition to security metrics and KPIs, organizations can also conduct periodic risk assessments and audits to evaluate the effectiveness of deployed controls. These assessments involve reviewing control implementations, testing control functionality, and identifying any gaps or deficiencies that may exist. One common approach to conducting risk assessments is through the use of vulnerability scanning tools, which scan systems and networks for known vulnerabilities and misconfigurations that could pose security risks. Organizations can use tools like Nessus or OpenVAS to scan their IT infrastructure for vulnerabilities and assess the effectiveness of implemented controls in mitigating those vulnerabilities.

Furthermore, organizations can leverage security information and event management (SIEM) solutions to monitor and analyze security events and incidents in real-time. SIEM platforms collect and correlate log data from various sources, such as network devices, servers, and applications, to detect suspicious activities and potential security breaches. By analyzing SIEM alerts and reports, organizations can identify anomalies, unauthorized access attempts, and other security-related events that may indicate control failures or weaknesses. Common SIEM platforms include Splunk, IBM QRadar, and Elasticsearch with the ELK Stack.

Another important aspect of monitoring risk controls effectiveness is conducting penetration testing and red team exercises to simulate real-world attack scenarios and assess the resilience of deployed controls. Penetration testing involves ethical hackers attempting to exploit vulnerabilities in systems and networks to identify potential security weaknesses and gaps in control implementations. Red team exercises take this a step further by simulating sophisticated cyberattacks and advanced persistent threats (APTs) to test the organization's detection and response capabilities. Organizations can use tools like

Metasploit or Cobalt Strike for penetration testing and engage third-party security firms to conduct red team exercises.

Moreover, organizations should establish incident response procedures and protocols to effectively respond to security incidents and breaches that may occur despite the implementation of preventive controls. Incident response plans outline the steps and actions to be taken in the event of a security incident, including incident detection, containment, eradication, and recovery. By regularly testing and updating incident response plans through tabletop exercises and simulations, organizations can ensure that their response procedures are effective and aligned with industry best practices.

Additionally, organizations can leverage threat intelligence feeds and information sharing platforms to stay informed about emerging threats, vulnerabilities, and attack techniques that may impact their risk controls effectiveness. Threat intelligence feeds provide real-time information about known threats and indicators of compromise (IOCs) that organizations can use to enhance their monitoring and detection capabilities. By integrating threat intelligence feeds into their security operations, organizations can proactively identify and respond to potential security risks before they escalate into full-blown incidents.

Furthermore, organizations should establish a continuous improvement mindset when it comes to monitoring and reviewing risk controls effectiveness. This involves regularly reviewing and updating control implementations, adjusting security configurations, and addressing any gaps or weaknesses identified through monitoring and assessment activities. By continuously refining their risk management practices and adapting to evolving threats and challenges, organizations can enhance their resilience and maintain a robust security posture in the face of an ever-changing threat landscape.

Chapter 7: Business Impact Analysis (BIA)

Conducting a Business Impact Analysis (BIA) is a crucial step in the development of a comprehensive business continuity and disaster recovery plan. A BIA assesses the potential impact of disruptions to critical business processes and identifies the resources and recovery strategies needed to minimize downtime and mitigate financial losses. To initiate a BIA, organizations typically assemble a cross-functional team consisting of representatives from various departments, including IT, operations, finance, and risk management. This team collaborates to identify and prioritize critical business processes and functions based on their importance to the organization's overall operations and objectives.

Once critical processes are identified, the next step in the BIA process is to assess the potential impacts of disruptions to these processes. This assessment involves analyzing the financial, operational, legal, regulatory, and reputational consequences of downtime or loss of functionality. To quantify the impact, organizations may use financial metrics such as revenue loss, cost of downtime, and potential fines or penalties for non-compliance with regulatory requirements. Operational metrics such as customer satisfaction, service level agreements (SLAs), and employee productivity can also be considered to assess the broader operational implications of disruptions.

To facilitate the BIA process, organizations often develop standardized questionnaires or surveys to gather information from key stakeholders within the organization. These questionnaires typically inquire about the criticality of specific business processes, dependencies on technology and infrastructure, recovery time objectives (RTOs), and acceptable levels of disruption. Stakeholder interviews and workshops may also be conducted to gather additional insights and perspectives on the potential impacts of disruptions.

Once data is collected and analyzed, the BIA team can prioritize critical business processes based on their impact on the organization's operations, financial stability, and reputation. This prioritization helps organizations focus their resources and efforts on developing effective continuity and recovery plans for the most essential functions. For example, a financial institution may prioritize the continuity of payment processing and customer account management systems due to the significant financial and reputational risks associated with downtime in these areas.

Following the identification and prioritization of critical processes, the BIA team works to define recovery objectives and strategies for each prioritized function. Recovery objectives specify the maximum tolerable downtime for each process, guiding the development of recovery plans and allocation of resources. Recovery strategies outline the specific actions and measures needed to restore functionality and minimize disruption in the event of a business interruption. These strategies may include backup and recovery procedures, redundant infrastructure, alternate work arrangements, and vendor agreements for outsourced services.

To validate and refine the proposed recovery strategies, organizations may conduct tabletop exercises or simulations to simulate various disaster scenarios and assess the effectiveness of response plans. These exercises help identify gaps in preparedness, test communication protocols, and familiarize key personnel with their roles and responsibilities during an actual incident. Based on the outcomes of these exercises, organizations can make adjustments to their recovery plans and allocate resources more effectively.

Additionally, organizations should regularly review and update their BIA findings and recovery plans to reflect changes in business processes, technology, regulations, and risk profiles. As the business environment evolves, new threats and vulnerabilities may emerge, requiring organizations to reassess their continuity and recovery strategies accordingly. By maintaining a proactive and iterative approach to BIA, organizations can enhance their resilience and readiness to respond effectively to disruptions and safeguard their business operations and assets.

Identifying critical business functions and dependencies is a foundational step in business continuity planning and risk management. This process involves identifying the key activities, processes, and systems that are essential for an organization's continued operation and success. To begin, organizations typically conduct a thorough assessment of their business operations to identify and prioritize critical functions. This assessment may involve engaging stakeholders from various departments to gain insights into the core activities that drive the organization's mission and objectives.

One common approach to identifying critical business functions is through a business impact analysis (BIA). A BIA evaluates the potential impact of disruptions to different business processes and helps organizations prioritize their recovery efforts based on the criticality of each function. During the BIA process, organizations assess factors such as the financial impact of downtime, the operational significance of specific processes, and the regulatory requirements that must be met.

Once critical business functions have been identified, the next step is to determine their dependencies. Dependencies are the relationships and connections between different elements of the business, including people, processes, technology, and external resources. Understanding these dependencies is crucial for developing effective continuity plans and ensuring that essential functions can be maintained during disruptions.

To identify dependencies, organizations may conduct interviews with key personnel, review documentation such as process maps and system diagrams, and analyze data flows within the organization. This process helps organizations identify the interdependencies between different business functions and the resources required to support them. For example, a critical business function like order processing may depend on various systems, including customer relationship management

(CRM) software, inventory management systems, and payment processing platforms.

In addition to internal dependencies, organizations must also consider external dependencies, such as relationships with suppliers, partners, and regulatory bodies. External dependencies can include reliance on third-party vendors for essential services, dependencies on critical infrastructure (e.g., utilities, telecommunications), and compliance requirements that must be met to maintain operations.

Once dependencies have been identified, organizations can assess the potential risks associated with each dependency and develop strategies to mitigate these risks. This may involve implementing redundancy measures, diversifying suppliers, establishing alternative communication channels, and creating contingency plans for different scenarios. For example, organizations may establish backup suppliers for critical components or establish contracts with multiple service providers to ensure continuity of essential services.

Furthermore, organizations should regularly review and update their assessments of critical functions and dependencies to reflect changes in the business environment. This includes changes in technology, regulations, market conditions, and organizational structure. By maintaining an up-to-date understanding of critical functions and dependencies, organizations can adapt their continuity plans and risk management strategies to address emerging threats and vulnerabilities.

In summary, identifying critical business functions and dependencies is a fundamental aspect of business continuity planning and risk management. By conducting thorough assessments and understanding the relationships between different elements of the business, organizations can develop robust continuity plans that enable them to withstand disruptions and maintain essential operations.

Chapter 8: Continuity of Operations Planning (COOP)

COOP planning, or Continuity of Operations Planning, is a crucial component of organizational resilience and disaster preparedness. It involves developing strategies and procedures to ensure that essential functions can continue during and after a wide range of disruptions, including natural disasters, cyber incidents, and other emergencies. COOP planning is essential for ensuring the continuity of critical operations, minimizing downtime, and mitigating the impact of disruptions on an organization's mission and objectives.

One key aspect of COOP planning is identifying and prioritizing critical functions and resources that are necessary for the organization's continued operation. This involves conducting a thorough assessment of the organization's operations, including its processes, systems, personnel, and dependencies. By identifying critical functions, organizations can focus their efforts on ensuring the continuity of these essential activities during disruptions.

Once critical functions have been identified, organizations can develop continuity plans to address various scenarios and contingencies. These plans outline the procedures, roles, and responsibilities for maintaining essential operations under adverse conditions. They may include measures such as relocating critical personnel to alternate facilities, implementing remote work arrangements, activating backup systems and infrastructure, and establishing communication protocols.

In addition to identifying critical functions and developing continuity plans, COOP planning also involves establishing communication channels and protocols for disseminating information during emergencies. This includes establishing procedures for notifying personnel, stakeholders, and other relevant parties about disruptions, recovery efforts, and changes to normal operations. Effective communication is essential for coordinating response efforts, maintaining situational awareness, and ensuring that everyone has the information they need to make informed decisions.

Another important aspect of COOP planning is testing and exercising continuity plans to ensure their effectiveness and readiness. This involves conducting tabletop exercises, simulations, and drills to validate the organization's response capabilities and identify areas for improvement. By testing continuity plans in a controlled environment, organizations can identify weaknesses, refine procedures, and build confidence in their ability to respond effectively to disruptions.

Furthermore, COOP planning requires ongoing monitoring, evaluation, and updating to ensure that plans remain current and effective. This includes regularly reviewing and revising continuity plans in response to changes in the organization's operations, environment, and risk landscape. It also involves conducting periodic assessments of the organization's resilience capabilities and identifying opportunities for improvement.

To deploy COOP planning effectively, organizations can use various tools and techniques to support the planning process. For example, they can use risk assessment methodologies to identify potential threats and vulnerabilities that could impact their operations. They can also use business impact analysis (BIA) to prioritize critical functions and resources based on their importance to the organization's mission and objectives. Additionally, organizations can leverage technology solutions to support COOP planning and execution. This may include using communication and collaboration tools to facilitate remote work and coordination during emergencies. It may also involve implementing cloud-based solutions for data backup and recovery to ensure that critical information remains accessible during disruptions.

Overall, COOP planning is essential for ensuring the resilience and continuity of operations in the face of various threats and disruptions. By identifying critical functions, developing continuity plans, establishing communication protocols, testing response capabilities, and regularly updating plans, organizations can enhance their ability to withstand and recover from emergencies. COOP planning is not only a best practice but also a critical component of effective risk management and business continuity.

Developing Continuity of Operations (COOP) strategies and procedures is a critical aspect of organizational resilience and disaster preparedness. COOP strategies involve identifying and prioritizing critical functions and resources necessary for an organization's continued operation during and after disruptions. These strategies aim to ensure the continuity of essential activities, minimize downtime, and mitigate the impact of disruptions on the organization's mission and objectives. To develop effective COOP strategies, organizations must first conduct a comprehensive assessment of their operations, including processes, systems, personnel, and dependencies. This assessment helps identify critical functions and resources that require special attention and protection in the event of an emergency.

Once critical functions have been identified, organizations can develop COOP procedures to address various scenarios and contingencies. These procedures outline the steps, roles, and responsibilities for maintaining essential operations under adverse conditions. They include measures such as relocating critical personnel to alternate facilities, activating backup systems and infrastructure, implementing remote work arrangements, and establishing communication protocols. COOP procedures also define the criteria for activating and deactivating continuity plans, as well as the process for coordinating response efforts across departments and teams.

In addition to developing COOP strategies and procedures, organizations must also establish communication channels and protocols to ensure timely and effective communication during emergencies. This includes establishing procedures for notifying personnel, stakeholders, and other relevant parties about disruptions, recovery efforts, and changes to normal operations. Effective communication is essential for coordinating response efforts, maintaining situational awareness, and ensuring that everyone has the information they need to make informed decisions.

To deploy COOP strategies and procedures effectively, organizations can use various tools and techniques to support the planning process. For example, they can use risk assessment methodologies to identify potential threats and vulnerabilities that could impact their operations. They can also use business impact analysis (BIA) to prioritize critical functions and resources based on their importance to the organization's mission and objectives. Additionally, organizations can leverage technology solutions to support COOP planning and execution. This may include using communication and collaboration tools to facilitate remote work and coordination during emergencies.

Once COOP strategies and procedures have been developed, organizations must test and exercise them regularly to ensure their effectiveness and readiness. This involves conducting tabletop exercises, simulations, and drills to validate response capabilities and identify areas for improvement. Testing also helps build confidence in the organization's ability to respond effectively to disruptions and ensures that personnel are familiar with their roles and responsibilities.

Furthermore, organizations must continuously monitor, evaluate, and update their COOP strategies and procedures to ensure that they remain current and effective. This includes regularly reviewing and revising plans in response to changes in the organization's operations, environment, and risk landscape. It also involves conducting periodic assessments of resilience capabilities and identifying opportunities for improvement.

Overall, developing COOP strategies and procedures is essential for ensuring the resilience and continuity of operations in the face of various threats and disruptions. By identifying critical functions, developing procedures, establishing communication protocols, testing response capabilities, and continuously monitoring and updating plans, organizations can enhance their ability to withstand and recover from emergencies. COOP planning is not only a best practice but also a critical component of effective risk management and business continuity.

Chapter 9: Disaster Recovery Planning (DRP)

Developing and implementing a Disaster Recovery Plan (DRP) is crucial for organizations to mitigate the impact of disasters and ensure business continuity in the face of disruptive events. A DRP outlines the procedures and strategies that an organization must follow to recover its IT infrastructure, data, and operations after a disaster or disruption. The first step in DRP development is to conduct a thorough risk assessment to identify potential threats and vulnerabilities that could affect the organization's ability to operate. This assessment helps prioritize risks and determine the most critical systems, applications, and data that require protection and recovery.

Once risks have been identified, organizations can begin developing the DRP by defining recovery objectives, strategies, and procedures. This involves establishing recovery time objectives (RTOs) and recovery point objectives (RPOs) for critical systems and data to guide the recovery process. RTO refers to the maximum acceptable downtime for systems and services, while RPO defines the maximum acceptable data loss in the event of a disruption.

Next, organizations must identify the resources, personnel, and technologies required to execute the DRP effectively. This may include identifying backup facilities, data centers, and cloud services to support recovery efforts. Organizations should also designate recovery teams and assign roles and responsibilities to ensure a coordinated response during emergencies.

To deploy the DRP, organizations must implement appropriate backup and recovery solutions to protect critical data and infrastructure. This may involve using backup software to create regular backups of data and systems and storing them in secure offsite locations. Organizations can use commands like "tar" or "rsync" in the command-line interface (CLI) to create and manage backups of files and directories. For example, the "tar" command can be used to create a compressed archive of files, while the "rsync" command can be used to synchronize files between different locations.

In addition to backups, organizations should implement redundancy and failover mechanisms to minimize downtime and ensure continuous availability of critical services. This may include deploying redundant servers, network connections, and power sources to maintain operations in the event of hardware or infrastructure failures.

Organizations should also establish procedures for testing and validating the DRP to ensure its effectiveness and readiness. This involves conducting regular drills, exercises, and simulations to validate recovery procedures, identify gaps, and train personnel. Testing the DRP helps build confidence in the organization's ability to recover from disasters and ensures that personnel are familiar with their roles and responsibilities.

Furthermore, organizations must regularly review and update the DRP to reflect changes in the organization's operations, technology, and risk landscape. This includes reviewing recovery objectives, procedures, and resources to ensure they remain current and aligned with business priorities. Organizations should also conduct post-incident reviews after any major disruption to identify lessons learned and opportunities for improvement.

In summary, developing and implementing a DRP is essential for organizations to mitigate the impact of disasters and ensure business continuity. By conducting risk assessments, defining recovery objectives, identifying resources, implementing backup and recovery solutions, testing procedures, and updating the plan regularly, organizations can enhance their resilience and ability to recover from disruptions. DRP deployment requires careful planning, coordination, and ongoing maintenance to ensure its effectiveness in safeguarding critical operations and data.

Testing and maintaining the effectiveness of a Disaster Recovery Plan (DRP) is paramount for organizations to ensure their readiness to respond to disasters and disruptions. Regular testing allows organizations to identify weaknesses in their DRP and address them before a real disaster occurs, minimizing downtime and data loss. There are various testing methods that organizations can employ to evaluate the effectiveness of their DRP, including tabletop exercises, walkthroughs, simulations, and full-scale drills.

Tabletop exercises involve scenario-based discussions where key stakeholders gather to review the DRP and discuss their roles and responsibilities in response to a simulated disaster scenario. These exercises help identify gaps in the plan, clarify communication channels, and ensure that personnel are familiar with their roles and procedures. During tabletop exercises, organizations can use commands like "grep" or "awk" in the command-line interface (CLI) to search log files, analyze system outputs, or parse configuration files for relevant information.

Walkthroughs are step-by-step reviews of the DRP to identify potential issues or gaps in the plan's implementation. This involves following the documented procedures and verifying that each step is clear, actionable, and well-defined. Walkthroughs help validate the completeness and accuracy of the DRP and ensure that all necessary resources and dependencies are accounted for. Organizations can use commands like "ls" or "cat" in the CLI to list files or display the contents of configuration files during walkthroughs.

Simulations involve conducting realistic scenarios to test the organization's response to a simulated disaster event. This may include simulating system failures, network outages, or data breaches to assess the organization's ability to execute the DRP under stress. Simulations allow organizations to evaluate the effectiveness of their recovery procedures, coordination among response teams, and communication with stakeholders. During simulations, organizations can use commands like "ping" or "traceroute" in the CLI to test network connectivity and identify potential issues.

Full-scale drills involve implementing the entire DRP in a controlled environment to simulate a real disaster response. This may include activating backup systems, relocating personnel to alternate sites, and restoring critical services to assess the organization's ability to recover from a major disruption. Full-scale drills help validate the organization's readiness to respond to disasters and identify areas for improvement in the DRP. Organizations can use commands like "rsync" or "scp" in the CLI to transfer files between systems or synchronize data during drills.

In addition to testing, maintaining the effectiveness of the DRP requires regular review and updates to ensure its alignment with changing business requirements, technology, and risk landscape. Organizations should conduct periodic reviews of the DRP to identify any changes in business processes, infrastructure, or dependencies that may impact the plan's effectiveness. This includes updating contact information, recovery procedures, and documentation to reflect the latest changes.

Furthermore, organizations should conduct post-incident reviews after any major disruption to assess the effectiveness of the DRP and identify lessons learned. This involves analyzing the organization's response to the incident, identifying strengths and weaknesses in the DRP, and implementing corrective actions to improve future response efforts. Post-incident reviews help organizations identify recurring issues, refine recovery procedures, and enhance their overall resilience to disasters.

In summary, testing and maintaining the effectiveness of the DRP is essential for organizations to ensure their readiness to respond to disasters and disruptions. By employing various testing methods, such as tabletop exercises, walkthroughs, simulations, and full-scale drills, organizations can validate the effectiveness of their recovery procedures, identify areas for improvement, and enhance their overall resilience. Regular review and updates to the DRP help ensure its alignment with evolving business needs and technology, while post-incident reviews enable organizations to learn from past experiences and continuously improve their disaster response capabilities.

Chapter 10: Compliance and Regulatory Considerations in Risk Management

Regulatory compliance frameworks provide guidelines and standards for organizations to ensure that they adhere to legal and industry-specific requirements related to data protection, privacy, security, and other areas. These frameworks are essential for organizations operating in regulated industries or handling sensitive data to mitigate risks, avoid legal penalties, and maintain trust with customers and stakeholders. One of the most well-known regulatory compliance frameworks is the Payment Card Industry Data Security Standard (PCI DSS), which is designed to protect cardholder data and prevent payment card fraud. Another widely adopted framework is the Health Insurance Portability and Accountability Act (HIPAA), which sets standards for the protection of sensitive patient health information.

Additionally, the General Data Protection Regulation (GDPR) is a comprehensive data protection law that applies to organizations operating within the European Union (EU) and regulates the processing of personal data. The GDPR imposes strict requirements on organizations regarding consent, data minimization, transparency, and accountability, with severe penalties for non-compliance. To comply with the GDPR, organizations must implement appropriate technical and organizational measures to ensure the security and privacy of personal data, conduct data protection impact assessments, and appoint a data protection officer.

Furthermore, the Sarbanes-Oxley Act (SOX) is a U.S. federal law that imposes stringent requirements on publicly traded companies to ensure accurate financial reporting and transparency. SOX mandates internal controls and procedures for financial reporting, including requirements for the assessment and disclosure of internal control weaknesses. Compliance with SOX involves implementing controls to safeguard financial data, ensuring the integrity of financial reporting processes, and conducting regular audits to assess compliance.

Moreover, the Federal Information Security Management Act (FISMA) is a U.S. federal law that establishes cybersecurity requirements for federal agencies and their contractors. FISMA requires federal agencies to develop, document, and implement risk-based cybersecurity programs to protect sensitive information and systems. Compliance with FISMA involves conducting regular risk assessments, implementing security controls, and reporting on the effectiveness of cybersecurity programs to oversight authorities.

Additionally, the International Organization for Standardization (ISO) publishes standards such as ISO/IEC 27001 and ISO/IEC 27002, which provide guidelines for establishing, implementing, maintaining, and continually improving information security management systems (ISMS). ISO 27001 is a certification standard that specifies the requirements for an ISMS, while ISO 27002 offers best practices for implementing security controls. Achieving ISO 27001 certification demonstrates an organization's commitment to information security and compliance with internationally recognized standards.

Furthermore, the National Institute of Standards and Technology (NIST) publishes cybersecurity frameworks such as the NIST Cybersecurity Framework (CSF), which provides a voluntary framework for improving cybersecurity risk management. The NIST CSF consists of core functions, categories, and subcategories that organizations can use to assess and improve their cybersecurity posture. It emphasizes the importance of identifying, protecting, detecting, responding to, and recovering from cybersecurity threats and incidents.

Moreover, industry-specific regulatory compliance frameworks exist for sectors such as healthcare, finance, energy, and telecommunications. For example, the Federal Financial Institutions Examination Council (FFIEC) issues guidelines for financial institutions to address risks related to information security, data privacy, and technology operations. Similarly, the North American Electric Reliability Corporation (NERC) develops standards for the reliability and security of the bulk power system in North America.

Additionally, compliance with regulatory frameworks often requires organizations to undergo audits and assessments conducted by internal or external auditors, regulatory agencies, or independent third-party assessors. These audits evaluate the organization's adherence to applicable laws, regulations, standards, and industry best practices. Organizations must provide evidence of compliance, such as policies, procedures, documentation, and evidence of control effectiveness, to demonstrate their commitment to regulatory compliance.

Furthermore, non-compliance with regulatory frameworks can result in significant consequences, including fines, legal liabilities, reputational damage, and loss of business opportunities. Therefore, organizations must prioritize compliance efforts and allocate resources to ensure that they meet regulatory requirements and mitigate associated risks. Compliance with regulatory frameworks is an ongoing process that requires continuous monitoring, review, and improvement to adapt to evolving threats, technologies, and regulatory changes.

Moreover, organizations can leverage technology solutions such as governance, risk, and compliance (GRC) platforms to streamline compliance efforts, automate processes, and centralize documentation and reporting. GRC platforms provide tools for risk assessment, policy management, control monitoring, audit management, and reporting, enabling organizations to manage compliance requirements more effectively and efficiently.

In summary, regulatory compliance frameworks play a crucial role in guiding organizations' efforts to protect sensitive information, maintain trust with stakeholders, and avoid legal and financial consequences. By adhering to regulatory requirements, organizations can demonstrate their commitment to security, privacy, and transparency, ultimately enhancing their overall resilience and competitiveness in the marketplace.

Integrating compliance requirements into risk management practices is essential for organizations to effectively identify, assess, and mitigate risks while ensuring adherence to applicable laws, regulations, and industry standards. One of the key aspects of this integration is understanding the regulatory landscape and identifying relevant compliance requirements that apply to the organization's operations and industry sector. This involves conducting thorough research and staying updated on changes to regulations, standards, and guidelines that may impact the organization's risk management processes.

Once the relevant compliance requirements have been identified, organizations must assess their existing risk management practices to determine how well they align with these requirements. This assessment may involve evaluating the organization's policies, procedures, controls, and governance structures to identify any gaps or deficiencies in addressing compliance obligations. For example, organizations may need to assess whether their risk assessment methodologies consider regulatory requirements and whether their risk mitigation strategies align with compliance mandates.

Following the assessment phase, organizations can develop a plan to integrate compliance requirements into their risk management practices. This plan should include specific actions and initiatives aimed at addressing identified gaps and enhancing the organization's ability to manage compliance-related risks effectively. For instance, organizations may need to update their risk assessment frameworks to include criteria for evaluating compliance risks or develop new policies and procedures to ensure adherence to regulatory requirements.

Moreover, technology can play a crucial role in integrating compliance requirements into risk management practices. Organizations can leverage GRC (governance, risk, and compliance) platforms to automate compliance monitoring, streamline risk assessment processes, and facilitate reporting and documentation. These platforms provide centralized repositories for storing compliance-related information, tracking regulatory changes, and managing compliance activities across the organization.

Furthermore, organizations should establish clear roles and responsibilities for managing compliance within the risk management framework. This may involve appointing a compliance officer or team responsible for overseeing compliance efforts, monitoring regulatory developments, and coordinating with relevant stakeholders to ensure alignment between risk management and compliance initiatives. Additionally, organizations may need to provide training and awareness programs to educate employees about compliance requirements and their role in supporting compliance efforts.

Another important aspect of integrating compliance requirements into risk management practices is establishing robust monitoring and reporting mechanisms to track compliance performance and identify emerging risks. This may involve implementing key risk indicators (KRIs) and key performance indicators (KPIs) to measure compliance effectiveness and risk exposure, as well as conducting regular audits and assessments to validate compliance with regulatory requirements.

Additionally, organizations should maintain open lines of communication with regulators, industry associations, and other stakeholders to stay informed about changes to compliance requirements and emerging trends in risk management. This may involve participating in industry forums, attending regulatory briefings, and engaging in dialogue with regulatory authorities to clarify compliance expectations and seek guidance on interpretation and implementation of regulations.

Furthermore, organizations should regularly review and update their risk management and compliance programs to reflect changes in the regulatory environment, business operations, and risk landscape. This iterative process of continuous improvement ensures that the organization remains agile and responsive to evolving compliance requirements and emerging risks.

In summary, integrating compliance requirements into risk management practices is essential for organizations to effectively identify, assess, and mitigate risks while ensuring adherence to applicable laws, regulations, and industry standards. By aligning risk management and compliance efforts, organizations can enhance their overall resilience and ability to navigate regulatory challenges while safeguarding their reputation and maintaining trust with stakeholders.

BOOK 4
ADVANCED SECURITY OPERATIONS
IMPLEMENTING SY0-701 BEST PRACTICES AND
BEYOND

ROB BOTWRIGHT

Chapter 1: Advanced Threat Detection Techniques

Behavioral analysis for threat detection involves the examination of patterns of behavior exhibited by users, devices, and systems to identify anomalies and potential security threats. One common approach to behavioral analysis is the use of machine learning algorithms to analyze large volumes of data and detect deviations from established baselines. For example, organizations can use anomaly detection algorithms to monitor network traffic, user activity, and system behavior for signs of suspicious or unauthorized activity. These algorithms learn from historical data to identify normal patterns of behavior and flag deviations that may indicate a security threat.

Another technique for behavioral analysis is user behavior analytics (UBA), which focuses on analyzing the actions and interactions of individual users to detect unusual or malicious behavior. UBA platforms collect and analyze data from various sources, such as log files, authentication logs, and application usage logs, to create profiles of normal user behavior. By comparing current behavior against these profiles, UBA systems can identify deviations indicative of insider threats, compromised accounts, or other security incidents.

Moreover, endpoint detection and response (EDR) solutions leverage behavioral analysis techniques to detect and respond to threats at the endpoint level. EDR agents deployed on endpoints continuously monitor system activity and behavior, looking for indicators of compromise (IOCs) and suspicious behavior patterns. When anomalies are detected, EDR systems can take automated actions, such as isolating the endpoint, blocking malicious processes, or alerting security teams for further investigation.

Furthermore, network traffic analysis (NTA) tools use behavioral analysis to identify abnormal network behavior that may indicate a security threat. These tools capture and analyze network traffic in real-time, looking for patterns of communication, data transfer, and access that deviate from normal network behavior. By correlating network activity with threat intelligence feeds and known attack patterns, NTA solutions can identify and block malicious activity before it causes harm to the network.

Additionally, cloud-based security solutions often incorporate behavioral analysis capabilities to detect threats across cloud environments and services. These solutions analyze user activity, access logs, and resource usage patterns to identify suspicious behavior indicative of account compromise, data exfiltration, or unauthorized access. By applying machine learning algorithms to large datasets, cloud security platforms can detect and respond to threats in real-time, helping organizations protect their cloud infrastructure and data.

Moreover, behavioral analysis can be applied to email security to detect phishing attacks, malware distribution, and other email-borne threats. Email security solutions use behavioral analysis techniques to analyze email content, sender behavior, and message headers to identify suspicious emails and prevent them from reaching users' inboxes. By examining patterns of email activity and communication, these solutions can identify anomalies indicative of phishing attempts or other malicious activity.

Furthermore, behavioral analysis can be used in combination with other security controls, such as intrusion detection systems (IDS) and security information and event management (SIEM) solutions, to enhance threat detection capabilities. By integrating behavioral analysis with these technologies, organizations can correlate security events and indicators across different sources to detect complex, multi-stage attacks and insider threats.

In summary, behavioral analysis is a powerful technique for threat detection that leverages machine learning algorithms, user behavior analytics, endpoint detection and response, network traffic analysis, and other technologies to identify anomalies and potential security threats. By continuously monitoring and analyzing patterns of behavior exhibited by users, devices, and systems, organizations can detect and respond to security incidents more effectively, reducing the risk of data breaches, network intrusions, and other cyber threats.

Machine learning algorithms play a crucial role in threat detection, enabling organizations to identify and respond to security threats more effectively. One of the key advantages of machine learning is its ability to analyze large volumes of data and identify patterns and anomalies that may indicate malicious activity. One commonly used machine learning technique in threat detection is supervised learning, where algorithms are trained on labeled datasets containing examples of both normal and malicious behavior. These algorithms learn to distinguish between benign and malicious activity based on the features present in the data. To deploy supervised learning algorithms for threat detection, organizations typically start by collecting labeled training data representative of normal and malicious behavior in their environment. They then use this data to train machine learning models using popular libraries such as scikit-learn or TensorFlow. For example, in the case of network intrusion detection, organizations can train supervised learning models to classify network traffic as either normal or malicious based on features such as source and destination IP addresses, port numbers, and packet payloads.

Another machine learning technique commonly used in threat detection is unsupervised learning, where algorithms are trained on unlabeled data to identify patterns and anomalies without prior knowledge of normal behavior. Unsupervised learning algorithms can be particularly useful for detecting novel or previously unseen threats that may not be captured by predefined rules or signatures. One popular unsupervised learning algorithm is clustering, where data points are grouped into clusters based on their similarity. For example, organizations can use clustering algorithms to group similar network traffic patterns together and identify outliers that may indicate suspicious activity.

Furthermore, anomaly detection is another machine learning approach used in threat detection, where algorithms are trained to identify deviations from normal behavior that may indicate a security threat. Anomaly detection algorithms learn to recognize patterns in the data and flag instances that deviate significantly from these patterns. To deploy anomaly detection techniques, organizations need to establish baseline models of normal behavior for various aspects of their environment, such as network traffic, user activity, and system behavior. They can then use anomaly detection algorithms to monitor these aspects for deviations from the baseline and generate alerts when anomalous behavior is detected.

Moreover, deep learning, a subset of machine learning, has emerged as a powerful technique for threat detection, particularly in the areas of image and text analysis. Deep learning models, such as convolutional neural networks (CNNs) and recurrent neural networks (RNNs), can learn complex patterns and relationships in data and make predictions based on this learning. For example, organizations can use deep learning models to analyze email content, web traffic, or malware samples and identify indicators of phishing attacks, malware infections, or other security threats.

Additionally, reinforcement learning, a form of machine learning where algorithms learn to make decisions by interacting with their environment, has shown promise in certain areas of threat detection, such as network security and malware analysis. In reinforcement learning, algorithms learn to maximize a reward signal by taking actions that lead to desirable outcomes. Organizations can deploy reinforcement learning algorithms to dynamically adapt their security controls and response strategies based on evolving threats and attack techniques.

Furthermore, ensemble learning techniques, which combine multiple machine learning models to improve predictive performance, are increasingly being used in threat detection. Ensemble methods such as random forests and gradient boosting combine the predictions of multiple base models to produce more robust and accurate results. By leveraging the diversity of multiple models, ensemble learning approaches can better capture the complexity of security threats and reduce false positives and false negatives.

In summary, machine learning algorithms are a valuable tool in threat detection, enabling organizations to analyze large volumes of data, identify patterns and anomalies, and respond to security threats more effectively. Whether using supervised learning, unsupervised learning, anomaly detection, deep learning, reinforcement learning, or ensemble learning techniques, organizations can leverage machine learning to enhance their security posture and protect against a wide range of cyber threats.

Chapter 2: Security Orchestration and Automation

Workflow automation in security operations is essential for streamlining processes, improving efficiency, and enhancing overall cybersecurity posture. By automating repetitive tasks and standardizing procedures, organizations can reduce manual errors, accelerate response times, and free up valuable resources to focus on more strategic initiatives. One common approach to workflow automation in security operations is through the use of scripting languages such as Python, PowerShell, or Bash. These languages provide powerful capabilities for automating tasks such as log analysis, incident response, and system configuration. For example, security analysts can use Python scripts to parse log files, extract relevant information, and generate alerts for suspicious activity. Similarly, PowerShell scripts can be used to automate common tasks in Windows environments, such as user account management, system configuration, and event log analysis.

Moreover, organizations can leverage configuration management tools such as Ansible, Puppet, or Chef to automate the deployment and management of security controls across their IT infrastructure. These tools allow security teams to define configuration policies in code and enforce them consistently across servers, workstations, and other devices. For instance, Ansible playbooks can be used to ensure that all systems are configured according to the organization's security standards, such as disabling unnecessary services, applying security patches, and enforcing strong password policies. Similarly, Puppet manifests or Chef recipes can be used to automate the installation and configuration of security software such as antivirus agents, intrusion detection systems, and firewalls.

Furthermore, workflow automation platforms such as ServiceNow, Jira, or Microsoft Power Automate provide organizations with the ability to design and automate complex workflows involving multiple teams and systems. These platforms offer visual workflow editors, pre-built integrations, and automation capabilities that enable security teams to orchestrate incident response processes, track security incidents, and collaborate effectively across the organization. For example, security analysts can use ServiceNow to create incident response workflows that automatically assign tasks to the appropriate teams, escalate critical incidents, and generate reports for management review.

Additionally, security orchestration, automation, and response (SOAR) platforms have emerged as powerful tools for automating and orchestrating security operations across the entire threat lifecycle. SOAR platforms integrate with a wide range of security tools and systems, such as SIEMs, endpoint detection and response (EDR) solutions, and threat intelligence feeds, allowing organizations to automate incident detection, investigation, and response processes. For example, a security analyst can use a SOAR platform to create playbooks that automate the response to specific types of security incidents, such as phishing attacks, ransomware infections, or data breaches. These playbooks can leverage predefined workflows, decision trees, and integrations with third-party tools to orchestrate a coordinated response across multiple security controls and systems.

Furthermore, the use of application programming interfaces (APIs) is another key enabler of workflow automation in security operations. APIs allow different security tools and systems to communicate and exchange data programmatically, enabling organizations to build custom integrations and automate workflows across disparate technologies. For example, security teams can use APIs to extract threat intelligence data from external sources, such as threat feeds or threat intelligence platforms, and integrate this data into their security operations workflows. Similarly, APIs can be used to automate the sharing of security information with external partners or customers, enabling organizations to collaborate more effectively on threat detection and response.

Moreover, the adoption of security automation and orchestration frameworks such as TheHive, Cortex, or Demisto allows organizations to leverage open-source tools and community-developed integrations to automate common security operations tasks. These frameworks provide a range of features and capabilities for incident management, threat intelligence analysis, and workflow automation, empowering security teams to respond to security incidents more efficiently and effectively. For example, security analysts can use TheHive to triage and investigate security alerts, while

Cortex can be used to enrich alerts with additional context from external threat intelligence sources.

Additionally, the use of robotic process automation (RPA) technology enables organizations to automate repetitive, rules-based tasks in security operations, such as data entry, report generation, and ticket handling. RPA software robots can mimic human actions within digital systems, allowing organizations to automate manual processes without making changes to existing IT infrastructure or applications. For example, security teams can use RPA bots to automatically log into security tools, collect and analyze data, and generate reports on security incidents or vulnerabilities.

Furthermore, the adoption of machine learning and artificial intelligence (AI) technologies is transforming security operations by enabling organizations to automate decision-making processes and detect complex threats more effectively. Machine learning algorithms can analyze large volumes of security data, identify patterns and anomalies, and generate predictive insights to help organizations proactively identify and respond to security threats. For example, AI-powered threat detection solutions can automatically analyze network traffic, user behavior, and endpoint activity to identify indicators of compromise and prioritize security alerts for investigation.

In summary, workflow automation is a critical component of modern security operations, enabling organizations to improve efficiency, reduce manual effort, and respond to security threats more effectively.

By leveraging scripting languages, configuration management tools, workflow automation platforms, SOAR platforms, APIs, open-source frameworks, RPA technology, and machine learning/AI technologies, organizations can automate and orchestrate security operations workflows across the entire threat lifecycle. This enables security teams to focus their time and resources on strategic activities such as threat hunting, incident response, and security analysis, ultimately enhancing the organization's overall cybersecurity posture.

The integration of security tools for orchestration plays a crucial role in streamlining security operations, enhancing efficiency, and improving overall cybersecurity posture within an organization. By seamlessly connecting various security tools and systems, organizations can automate repetitive tasks, orchestrate complex workflows, and facilitate better collaboration between different security teams and technologies. One common approach to integrating security tools for orchestration is through the use of application programming interfaces (APIs). APIs allow different security tools to communicate and exchange data programmatically, enabling organizations to build custom integrations and automate workflows across disparate technologies. For example, security teams can use APIs to extract threat intelligence data from external sources, such as threat feeds or threat intelligence platforms, and integrate this data into their security operations workflows. Similarly, APIs can be used to automate the sharing of security information with external partners or customers, enabling organizations to collaborate more effectively on threat detection and response.

Moreover, security orchestration, automation, and response (SOAR) platforms have emerged as powerful tools for integrating and orchestrating security tools and systems across the entire threat lifecycle. SOAR platforms provide organizations with a centralized platform for managing security operations, automating incident response processes, and orchestrating workflows involving multiple security tools and technologies. These platforms offer built-in integrations with a wide range of security tools, such as SIEMs, endpoint detection and response (EDR) solutions, and threat intelligence feeds, allowing organizations to automate incident detection, investigation, and response processes. For example, a security analyst can use a SOAR platform to create playbooks that automate the response to specific types of security incidents, such as phishing attacks, ransomware infections, or data breaches. These playbooks can leverage predefined workflows, decision trees, and integrations with third-party tools to orchestrate a coordinated response across multiple security controls and systems.

Furthermore, organizations can leverage security information and event management (SIEM) solutions to integrate and correlate security data from various sources, providing a centralized view of security events and incidents. SIEM solutions collect and analyze log data from network devices, servers, applications, and other sources, allowing organizations to detect and respond to security threats in real-time. By integrating SIEM solutions with other security tools and systems, organizations can automate incident detection and response processes, correlate security events across different data sources, and prioritize security alerts for investigation. For example, a SIEM solution can ingest log data from firewalls, intrusion detection systems (IDS), and antivirus solutions, correlate this data to identify patterns and anomalies indicative of a security breach, and generate alerts for further investigation.

Additionally, organizations can leverage security automation platforms such as Phantom, Swimlane, or Demisto to orchestrate security tools and automate incident response processes. These platforms provide organizations with a range of features and capabilities for automating security operations workflows, such as incident enrichment, investigation, and response. For example, security analysts can use a security automation platform to create playbooks that automate the response to specific types of security incidents, such as malware infections, phishing attacks, or insider threats. These playbooks can leverage predefined workflows, integrations with third-party tools, and decision trees to orchestrate a coordinated response across multiple security controls and systems.

Moreover, the adoption of open-source security orchestration frameworks such as TheHive, Cortex, or MISP enables organizations to leverage community-developed integrations and workflows to orchestrate security tools and automate incident response processes. These frameworks provide organizations with a range of features and capabilities for incident management, threat intelligence analysis, and workflow automation, empowering security teams to respond to security incidents more efficiently and effectively. For example, security analysts can use TheHive to triage and investigate security alerts, while Cortex can be used to enrich alerts with additional context from external threat intelligence sources.

Furthermore, the use of security analytics platforms such as Splunk, ELK Stack (Elasticsearch, Logstash, Kibana), or IBM QRadar enables organizations to integrate and analyze security data from various sources, such as log files, network traffic, and endpoint logs, to detect and respond to security threats more effectively. These platforms provide organizations with advanced analytics capabilities, such as machine learning, anomaly detection, and behavioral analytics, allowing them to identify patterns and anomalies indicative of a security breach. By integrating security analytics platforms with other security tools and systems, organizations can automate incident detection and response processes, correlate security events across different data sources, and prioritize security alerts for investigation.

In summary, the integration of security tools for orchestration is essential for streamlining security operations, automating incident response processes, and improving overall cybersecurity posture within an organization. By leveraging APIs, SOAR platforms, SIEM solutions, security automation platforms, open-source orchestration frameworks, and security analytics platforms, organizations can integrate and orchestrate security tools and systems across the entire threat lifecycle. This enables security teams to respond to security incidents more efficiently and effectively, reducing the time to detect and mitigate security threats and minimizing the impact of security breaches on the organization.

Chapter 3: Incident Response Optimization

Incident response plan enhancement is a critical aspect of cybersecurity strategy aimed at optimizing an organization's ability to detect, respond to, and recover from security incidents effectively. One key aspect of enhancing an incident response plan is to regularly review and update it to reflect changes in the threat landscape, technology infrastructure, regulatory requirements, and organizational priorities. Organizations can use various techniques and strategies to enhance their incident response plans, including conducting tabletop exercises, performing post-incident reviews, leveraging threat intelligence, and integrating automation and orchestration capabilities. Tabletop exercises are a valuable technique for testing and refining an organization's incident response plan in a controlled environment. During tabletop exercises, key stakeholders, including members of the incident response team, executive leadership, legal counsel, and IT staff, simulate different types of security incidents and work together to assess the effectiveness of the response plan and identify areas for improvement. These exercises help organizations identify gaps in their incident response processes, evaluate the coordination and communication among different teams, and validate the effectiveness of existing controls and procedures. Additionally, organizations can leverage post-incident reviews to analyze the response to actual security incidents, identify lessons learned, and implement corrective actions to prevent similar incidents in the future. By conducting thorough post-incident reviews, organizations can gain valuable insights into the effectiveness of their incident response plan, identify areas for improvement, and refine their incident response processes accordingly. Another important strategy for enhancing an incident response plan is to leverage threat intelligence to proactively identify and mitigate security threats. Threat intelligence provides organizations with valuable insights into emerging threats, attacker tactics, techniques, and procedures (TTPs), and indicators of compromise (IOCs) that can help inform incident detection and response efforts. Organizations can use threat intelligence feeds, reports, and analysis to enrich their incident detection capabilities, improve their understanding of the threat landscape, and prioritize their response efforts based on the severity and relevance of identified threats. Moreover, integrating automation and orchestration capabilities into an incident response plan can significantly enhance its effectiveness and efficiency. Automation and orchestration technologies allow organizations to automate repetitive tasks, streamline incident response workflows, and accelerate the time to detect and respond to security incidents. By leveraging automation and orchestration capabilities, organizations can improve their ability to detect and contain security incidents in real-time, reduce the manual effort required to respond to incidents, and minimize the impact of security breaches on the organization. Organizations can deploy automation and orchestration capabilities using specialized platforms and tools that offer features such as workflow automation, playbook creation, alert enrichment, and integration with security tools and systems. These platforms enable organizations to build custom workflows and playbooks that automate incident response processes, integrate with existing security tools and systems, and orchestrate a coordinated response across the entire organization. Additionally, organizations can leverage security orchestration, automation, and response (SOAR) platforms to centralize incident response activities, automate repetitive tasks, and orchestrate workflows involving multiple security tools and technologies. SOAR platforms provide organizations with a unified platform for managing security incidents, automating response processes, and orchestrating actions across different security controls and systems. By integrating SOAR capabilities into their incident response plan, organizations can improve their ability to detect, investigate, and respond to security incidents more effectively, minimize the impact of security breaches, and enhance their overall cybersecurity posture. In summary, incident response plan enhancement is essential for organizations to effectively detect, respond to, and recover from security incidents. By regularly reviewing and updating their incident response plans, conducting tabletop exercises, performing post-incident reviews, leveraging threat intelligence, and integrating automation and orchestration capabilities, organizations can enhance their incident response capabilities, improve their ability to detect and respond to security incidents, and minimize the impact of security breaches on the organization.

Incident triage and prioritization strategies are fundamental components of an effective incident response plan, enabling organizations to efficiently manage and respond to security incidents based on their severity, impact, and urgency. One common approach to incident triage and prioritization is the use of a triage matrix or scoring system to assess the criticality of each incident and determine the appropriate response. Organizations can develop their triage matrices based on factors such as the type of incident, the systems or data affected, the potential impact on business operations, and regulatory compliance requirements. By assigning a score or priority level to each incident based on these criteria, organizations can prioritize their response efforts and allocate resources effectively to address the most critical incidents first. Another strategy for incident triage and prioritization is the use of incident categorization and classification frameworks, such as the Common Vulnerability Scoring System (CVSS) or the Common Vulnerability and Exposures (CVE) database, to classify incidents based on their severity and potential impact. These frameworks provide standardized criteria for assessing the severity of security vulnerabilities and incidents, enabling organizations to prioritize their response efforts based on the level of risk posed by each incident. Additionally, organizations can leverage automated incident triage and prioritization tools and technologies to streamline the process of assessing and prioritizing security incidents. These tools use machine learning algorithms and analytics to analyze incident data, identify patterns and trends, and assign priority levels to incidents based on predefined criteria. By automating the triage and prioritization process, organizations can reduce the time and effort required to assess incidents manually, improve response times, and ensure that critical incidents are addressed promptly. Furthermore, organizations can implement incident response playbooks and workflows that define predefined response actions and escalation procedures for different types of incidents. These playbooks outline the steps that should be followed to contain, investigate, and remediate security incidents based on their severity and impact. By defining clear and actionable response procedures in advance, organizations can streamline the incident response process, ensure consistency in their response efforts, and minimize the risk of human error during high-pressure situations. Incident response playbooks can be created using specialized incident management platforms or through manual documentation, and should be regularly reviewed and updated to reflect changes in the threat landscape, technology infrastructure, and regulatory requirements. Moreover, organizations can leverage threat intelligence feeds and indicators of compromise (IOCs) to prioritize their response efforts based on the likelihood of an incident being part of a larger-scale attack or campaign. By correlating incident data with threat intelligence, organizations can identify patterns and trends that may indicate a more significant threat and prioritize their response efforts accordingly. Additionally, organizations can use real-time monitoring and alerting capabilities to identify and prioritize incidents as they occur. By implementing continuous monitoring solutions and leveraging security information and event management (SIEM) platforms, organizations can detect and prioritize incidents in real-time based on predefined alerting thresholds and criteria. These solutions enable organizations to proactively identify and respond to security incidents before they escalate, minimizing the potential impact on business operations. In summary, incident triage and prioritization strategies are essential for organizations to effectively manage and respond to security incidents. By leveraging triage matrices, classification frameworks, automated tools and technologies, incident response playbooks, threat intelligence, and real-time monitoring capabilities, organizations can prioritize their response efforts, allocate resources effectively, and minimize the impact of security incidents on the organization.

Chapter 4: Proactive Security Monitoring Strategies

Threat hunting methodologies encompass a proactive approach to cybersecurity that involves actively seeking out and identifying potential threats within an organization's network and systems, rather than waiting for them to be detected by traditional security measures. One commonly used threat hunting methodology is the "Hunt Team" approach, where dedicated teams of security analysts are tasked with conducting continuous hunts for potential threats and indicators of compromise (IOCs) within an organization's network and systems. These teams utilize a variety of techniques and tools to search for suspicious behavior, anomalous activity, and known attack patterns that may indicate the presence of a threat actor or malware. Another threat hunting methodology is the "Adversary Emulation" approach, which involves simulating the tactics, techniques, and procedures (TTPs) of real-world threat actors to identify weaknesses in an organization's defenses and improve its ability to detect and respond to advanced threats. This approach typically involves conducting red team exercises, penetration tests, and simulated cyber attacks to assess an organization's security posture and identify areas for improvement. Additionally, threat hunting methodologies often incorporate the use of threat intelligence feeds and indicators of compromise (IOCs) to prioritize hunting efforts and focus on the most relevant and high-priority threats. These feeds provide valuable information about emerging threats, known attack patterns, and indicators of compromise that can help threat hunters identify and mitigate potential risks more effectively. Furthermore, threat hunting methodologies may involve the use of advanced analytics and machine learning algorithms to analyze large volumes of data and identify patterns and anomalies that may indicate the presence of a threat. These techniques enable threat hunters to sift through vast amounts of data more efficiently and identify potential threats more quickly, allowing them to respond more effectively and minimize the impact of cyber attacks. Moreover, threat hunting methodologies often incorporate the use of behavioral analysis techniques to identify abnormal or suspicious behavior within an organization's network and systems. By monitoring user and system activity and looking for deviations from normal behavior patterns, threat hunters can identify potential indicators of compromise (IOCs) and proactively investigate them before they escalate into full-blown security incidents. Additionally, threat hunting methodologies may involve the use of honeypots and decoy systems to lure potential attackers into revealing their tactics and techniques. By deploying these deceptive systems within an organization's network, threat hunters can gather valuable intelligence about the tactics and techniques used by threat actors and use this information to improve their threat hunting efforts and strengthen their defenses. Furthermore, threat hunting methodologies often involve the use of automated tools and technologies to streamline the threat hunting process and improve efficiency. These tools can help threat hunters collect and analyze data more quickly, identify potential threats more accurately, and respond to incidents more effectively, ultimately enhancing an organization's overall security posture. In summary, threat hunting methodologies play a crucial role in modern cybersecurity by enabling organizations to proactively identify and mitigate potential threats before they can cause harm. By incorporating a combination of techniques, tools, and technologies, threat hunters can detect and respond to advanced threats more effectively, strengthen their security defenses, and protect their organizations from cyber attacks.

Predictive analytics for security monitoring involves the use of advanced statistical algorithms and machine learning techniques to analyze data and identify potential security threats before they occur. One of the primary goals of predictive analytics in security monitoring is to detect patterns and anomalies in data that may indicate the presence of a security threat or potential breach. This approach enables organizations to take proactive measures to prevent security incidents and mitigate risks before they escalate into major security breaches. One common technique used in predictive analytics for security monitoring is anomaly detection, which involves identifying deviations from normal patterns of behavior within an organization's network and systems. By analyzing historical data and identifying trends and patterns, anomaly detection algorithms can identify unusual behavior that may indicate a security threat, such as unauthorized access attempts or unusual network traffic patterns. Another important aspect of predictive analytics for security monitoring is the use of machine learning algorithms to analyze data and identify potential threats. Machine learning algorithms can analyze large volumes of data and identify patterns and correlations that may not be apparent to human analysts. By training machine learning models on historical data and feeding them new data in real-time, organizations can detect and respond to security threats more quickly and effectively. One example of predictive analytics for security monitoring is the use of machine learning algorithms to analyze user behavior and identify potential insider threats. By analyzing data such as user login patterns, access permissions, and file access history, machine learning algorithms can identify users who may pose a risk to the organization's security and alert security teams to take action. Additionally, predictive analytics can be used to identify emerging threats and vulnerabilities before they are exploited by attackers. By analyzing data from sources such as threat intelligence feeds, vulnerability databases, and security logs, organizations can identify trends and patterns that may indicate the presence of new security threats or vulnerabilities. For example, organizations can use predictive analytics to analyze patterns in malware distribution and identify new malware strains before they infect systems. Furthermore, predictive analytics can be used to improve the efficiency and effectiveness of security monitoring by automating the analysis of security data and prioritizing alerts based on their likelihood of being a genuine security threat. By using machine learning algorithms to analyze security data and identify high-risk events, organizations can reduce the workload of security analysts and focus their efforts on investigating the most critical security incidents. Additionally, predictive analytics can help organizations identify weaknesses in their security defenses and prioritize remediation efforts based on their potential impact on the organization's security posture. For example, organizations can use predictive analytics to identify vulnerabilities in their network infrastructure and prioritize patching efforts based on the severity of the vulnerabilities and their potential impact on the organization's operations. Overall, predictive analytics for security monitoring is a powerful tool for identifying and mitigating security threats before they can cause harm to an organization. By analyzing data in real-time and identifying patterns and anomalies that may indicate a security threat, organizations can take proactive measures to protect their systems and data from cyber attacks.

Chapter 5: Adaptive Security Architecture

Dynamic Defense Frameworks are comprehensive strategies designed to adapt and respond to evolving cybersecurity threats in real-time, offering organizations a proactive approach to security. These frameworks encompass a range of proactive measures, including threat detection, incident response, and threat intelligence integration, to enhance an organization's resilience against cyber threats. One essential component of dynamic defense frameworks is continuous monitoring of network activity and system logs using tools like Security Information and Event Management (SIEM) platforms. SIEM platforms aggregate and analyze log data from various sources across the network, allowing security teams to detect and respond to suspicious activity promptly. Implementing a dynamic defense framework often involves deploying intrusion detection and prevention systems (IDPS) to monitor network traffic for signs of unauthorized access or malicious activity. IDPS solutions use a combination of signature-based detection, anomaly detection, and behavioral analysis to identify and block potential threats in real-time. Additionally, dynamic defense frameworks emphasize the importance of threat intelligence integration, allowing organizations to leverage external threat intelligence feeds to enhance their understanding of emerging threats and vulnerabilities. Threat intelligence feeds provide valuable information about the tactics, techniques, and procedures (TTPs) used by threat actors, enabling organizations to proactively defend against known threats. Another key aspect of dynamic defense frameworks is the use of automation and orchestration to streamline security operations and response processes. Automation tools can help organizations automate repetitive tasks such as vulnerability scanning, patch management, and incident response, allowing security teams to focus on more strategic security initiatives. Deploying dynamic defense frameworks also involves implementing proactive measures to prevent security incidents before they occur. This may include implementing robust access controls, conducting regular security awareness training for employees, and performing regular security assessments to identify and address potential vulnerabilities in the organization's infrastructure. Additionally, dynamic defense frameworks prioritize incident response preparedness, ensuring that organizations have effective incident response plans and procedures in place to respond quickly and effectively to security incidents. This may involve conducting regular incident response exercises and simulations to test the organization's ability to detect, contain, and mitigate security threats. Furthermore, dynamic defense frameworks emphasize the importance of collaboration and information sharing within the cybersecurity community. By participating in information-sharing initiatives such as Information Sharing and Analysis Centers (ISACs) and industry-specific threat intelligence sharing groups, organizations can gain valuable insights into emerging threats and trends, enabling them to strengthen their defenses accordingly. Continuous improvement is also a fundamental principle of dynamic defense frameworks, with organizations regularly reviewing and updating their security policies, procedures, and controls to adapt to evolving threats and technologies. This may involve conducting regular security assessments and audits to identify areas for improvement and implementing measures to address any identified weaknesses. Overall, dynamic defense frameworks provide organizations with a proactive and adaptive approach to cybersecurity, enabling them to stay ahead of emerging threats and protect their critical assets effectively. By combining continuous monitoring, threat intelligence integration, automation, and proactive security measures, organizations can strengthen their defenses and reduce their risk of falling victim to cyber attacks.

Cloud security best practices are essential for ensuring the protection of data, applications, and infrastructure in cloud environments. These practices encompass a range of strategies and techniques designed to mitigate risks and vulnerabilities associated with cloud computing. One fundamental aspect of cloud security best practices is implementing strong identity and access management (IAM) controls to manage user permissions and access privileges. IAM solutions enable organizations to authenticate and authorize users, control their access to resources, and enforce security policies. For example, using AWS Identity and Access Management (IAM), organizations can create IAM users, groups, and roles to manage access to AWS services and resources. They can assign permissions to IAM entities using policies, which define what actions users can perform on which resources. By implementing IAM controls, organizations can ensure that only authorized users have access to cloud resources and data, reducing the risk of unauthorized access and data breaches. Another critical aspect of cloud security best practices is encrypting data both at rest and in transit to protect it from unauthorized access and interception. Encryption ensures that even if attackers gain access to cloud storage or network traffic, they cannot read or decipher the data without the encryption keys. Cloud service providers offer encryption capabilities for data storage and communication channels, allowing organizations to encrypt sensitive data before storing it in the cloud or transmitting it over the network. For example, AWS offers server-side encryption for data stored in Amazon S3 buckets, which encrypts data using AES-256 encryption before storing it in the cloud. Additionally, organizations can use SSL/TLS encryption to secure data transmission between clients and cloud services, ensuring that data remains confidential and secure during transit. Implementing encryption controls helps organizations comply with regulatory requirements and industry standards while protecting sensitive data from unauthorized access and disclosure. Another essential practice in cloud security is implementing network security controls to protect cloud environments from external and internal threats. This includes configuring firewalls, intrusion detection and prevention systems (IDPS), and network segmentation to control traffic flow and detect suspicious activity. Cloud service providers offer native network security features that organizations can use to protect their cloud environments. For example, AWS provides security groups and network access control lists (NACLs) to control inbound and outbound traffic to EC2 instances and VPCs. Organizations can configure security groups to allow or deny specific types of traffic based on source IP addresses, ports, and protocols, while NACLs provide an additional layer of security by filtering traffic at the subnet level. By configuring network security controls, organizations can reduce the attack surface and prevent unauthorized access to cloud resources and data. Additionally, implementing logging and monitoring practices is crucial for detecting and responding to security incidents in cloud environments. Cloud service providers offer logging and monitoring tools that organizations can use to track user activity, monitor system performance, and detect security threats. For example, AWS CloudTrail provides a comprehensive audit trail of API calls made within an AWS account, allowing organizations to track changes to resources, identify security misconfigurations, and investigate security incidents. Similarly, AWS CloudWatch enables organizations to monitor AWS resources and applications in real-time, set up alarms for specific events, and collect logs and metrics for analysis. By analyzing log data and monitoring system activity, organizations can detect signs of unauthorized access, data breaches, or other security incidents and take immediate action to mitigate the risk. Implementing regular security audits and assessments is also critical for ensuring compliance with regulatory requirements and identifying security gaps in cloud environments. Organizations should conduct regular vulnerability scans, penetration tests, and compliance audits to assess the security posture of their cloud infrastructure and applications. These assessments help identify vulnerabilities, misconfigurations, and compliance issues that could expose the organization to security risks. For example, organizations can use tools like AWS Inspector to automate security assessments of EC2 instances, identifying common security vulnerabilities and compliance violations. Similarly, third-party security vendors offer cloud security assessment services that organizations can use to evaluate the effectiveness of their security controls and identify areas for improvement. By conducting regular security audits and assessments, organizations can identify and remediate security vulnerabilities proactively, reducing the likelihood of security breaches and compliance violations. In summary, implementing cloud security best practices is essential for protecting data, applications, and infrastructure in cloud environments. By implementing strong identity and access management controls, encrypting data, implementing network security controls, logging and monitoring system activity, and conducting regular security audits and assessments, organizations can mitigate security risks and ensure the security and compliance of their cloud environments. These practices help organizations build a robust security posture in the cloud, protecting against a wide range of cyber threats and ensuring the confidentiality, integrity, and availability of their data and resources.

Chapter 6: Cloud Security Operations

Securing cloud-native applications is a critical aspect of modern cybersecurity, given the increasing adoption of cloud computing and the widespread use of cloud-native architectures and technologies. Cloud-native applications are designed to run in cloud environments, leveraging cloud-native services, containers, microservices, and serverless computing models. Securing these applications requires a comprehensive approach that addresses various aspects of security, including identity and access management, data protection, network security, application security, and compliance. One fundamental aspect of securing cloud-native applications is implementing strong identity and access management (IAM) controls to manage user access and permissions effectively. IAM solutions allow organizations to authenticate and authorize users, control their access to resources, and enforce security policies based on roles and permissions. For example, using AWS Identity and Access Management (IAM), organizations can create IAM users, groups, and roles to manage access to AWS services and resources. They can assign fine-grained permissions to IAM entities using IAM policies, which define what actions users can perform on which resources. By implementing IAM controls, organizations can ensure that only authorized users have access to cloud resources and data, reducing the risk of unauthorized access and data breaches.

Another critical aspect of securing cloud-native applications is implementing data protection mechanisms to safeguard sensitive data from unauthorized access and disclosure. This includes encrypting data both at rest and in transit, implementing data loss prevention (DLP) controls, and managing encryption keys securely. Cloud service providers offer encryption capabilities for data storage and communication channels, allowing organizations to encrypt sensitive data before storing it in the cloud or transmitting it over the network. For example, AWS offers server-side encryption for data stored in Amazon S3 buckets, which encrypts data using AES-256 encryption before storing it in the cloud. Additionally, organizations can use SSL/TLS encryption to secure data transmission between clients and cloud services, ensuring that data remains confidential and secure during transit. Implementing encryption controls helps organizations comply with regulatory requirements and industry standards while protecting sensitive data from unauthorized access and disclosure. Network security is another critical aspect of securing cloud-native applications, as it helps protect cloud environments from external and internal threats. Organizations should implement network security controls such as firewalls, intrusion detection and prevention systems (IDPS), and network segmentation to control traffic flow and detect suspicious activity. Cloud service providers offer native network security features that organizations can use to protect their cloud environments. For example, AWS provides security groups and network access control lists (NACLs) to control inbound and outbound traffic to EC2 instances and VPCs. Organizations can configure security groups to allow or deny specific types of traffic based on source IP addresses, ports, and protocols, while NACLs provide an additional layer of security by filtering traffic at the subnet level. By configuring network security controls, organizations can reduce the attack surface and prevent unauthorized access to cloud resources and data. Application security is another critical consideration when securing cloud-native applications, as vulnerabilities in application code or configuration can expose organizations to security risks. Organizations should follow secure coding practices, conduct regular security assessments and code reviews, and implement runtime application security controls to protect against common threats such as injection attacks, cross-site scripting (XSS), and insecure deserialization. For example, organizations can use AWS WAF (Web Application Firewall) to protect web applications running on AWS from common web exploits and security vulnerabilities. AWS WAF allows organizations to create rules that filter web traffic based on conditions such as IP addresses, HTTP headers, and request parameters, allowing them to block malicious traffic and protect their applications from attacks. Additionally, organizations should implement security monitoring and logging solutions to detect and respond to security incidents in real-time. Cloud-native applications generate a vast amount of log data, including application logs, system logs, and network logs, which can be analyzed to identify signs of unauthorized access, data breaches, or other security incidents. Cloud service providers offer logging and monitoring tools that organizations can use to track user activity, monitor system performance, and detect security threats. For example, AWS CloudTrail provides a comprehensive audit trail of API calls made within an AWS account, allowing organizations to track changes to resources, identify security misconfigurations, and investigate security incidents. Similarly, AWS CloudWatch enables organizations to monitor AWS resources and applications in real-time, set up alarms for specific events, and collect logs and metrics for analysis. By analyzing log data and monitoring system activity, organizations can detect signs of unauthorized access, data breaches, or other security incidents and take immediate action to mitigate the risk. In summary, securing cloud-native applications requires a comprehensive approach that addresses various aspects of security, including identity and access management, data protection, network security, application security, and compliance. By implementing strong security controls, following secure coding practices, conducting regular security assessments, and implementing security monitoring and logging solutions, organizations can protect their cloud-native applications from a wide range of security threats and ensure the confidentiality, integrity, and availability of their data and resources.

Chapter 7: Insider Threat Mitigation

Insider threat detection technologies play a crucial role in identifying and mitigating internal security risks within organizations. These technologies are designed to monitor user activities, detect abnormal behavior, and identify potential insider threats before they cause harm to the organization. One of the primary methods used in insider threat detection is user behavior analytics (UBA), which involves analyzing user activities and behavior patterns to identify anomalies or suspicious behavior. UBA solutions collect and analyze data from various sources, such as log files, network traffic, and user activity logs, to establish a baseline of normal behavior for each user and detect deviations from that baseline. By using machine learning algorithms and statistical models, UBA solutions can identify potential insider threats based on deviations from normal behavior, such as accessing sensitive data at unusual times or locations, downloading large amounts of data, or exhibiting unusual patterns of communication. Another essential technology in insider threat detection is data loss prevention (DLP), which focuses on preventing unauthorized access to sensitive data and preventing data breaches caused by insiders. DLP solutions use a combination of content analysis, contextual analysis, and policy-based controls to monitor and control the movement of sensitive data within the organization. By classifying data based on its sensitivity level and applying policies to restrict access and prevent unauthorized sharing or exfiltration, DLP solutions can help organizations protect their sensitive information from insider threats. Additionally, endpoint detection and response (EDR) solutions play a critical role in insider threat detection by monitoring endpoint devices, such as desktops, laptops, and servers, for signs of malicious activity or unauthorized access. EDR solutions collect and analyze telemetry data from endpoint devices, such as process execution, file system activity, and network connections, to detect indicators of compromise (IOCs) and suspicious behavior. By correlating endpoint telemetry data with threat intelligence feeds and behavioral analytics, EDR solutions can identify potential insider threats and respond to security incidents in real-time. Privileged access management (PAM) solutions are also essential for insider threat detection, as insiders with privileged access pose a significant risk to organizations due to their elevated permissions and access to sensitive resources. PAM solutions help organizations manage and monitor privileged accounts and access rights, enforce least privilege principles, and detect and respond to unauthorized or suspicious activities performed by privileged users. By implementing PAM controls, organizations can reduce the risk of insider threats and prevent unauthorized access to critical systems and data. Insider threat detection technologies also include user activity monitoring (UAM) solutions, which capture and analyze user interactions with IT systems and applications to detect potential insider threats and policy violations. UAM solutions record user sessions, keystrokes, commands, and application activities, allowing organizations to monitor and audit user behavior in real-time. By analyzing user activity logs and correlating them with other security events and indicators, UAM solutions can detect suspicious behavior, such as unauthorized access attempts, data exfiltration, or policy violations, and alert security teams to potential insider threats. In summary, insider threat detection technologies play a critical role in helping organizations identify and mitigate internal security risks posed by insiders. By leveraging technologies such as user behavior analytics, data loss prevention, endpoint detection and response, privileged access management, and user activity monitoring, organizations can detect and respond to insider threats in real-time, protect sensitive data and resources, and safeguard against the potentially devastating impact of insider attacks.

Behavioral analysis for insider threat prevention involves the use of advanced techniques to monitor, analyze, and identify suspicious behavior patterns exhibited by employees or other insiders within an organization. These techniques leverage machine learning algorithms, statistical models, and data analytics to detect anomalies in user behavior and identify potential insider threats before they can cause harm to the organization. One common approach to behavioral analysis for insider threat prevention is user behavior analytics (UBA), which focuses on monitoring and analyzing user activities and behavior patterns to detect deviations from normal behavior. UBA solutions collect data from various sources, such as log files, network traffic, and user activity logs, and use advanced analytics to establish a baseline of normal behavior for each user. By comparing individual user behavior to this baseline, UBA solutions can identify anomalies or deviations that may indicate potential insider threats. For example, if a user suddenly starts accessing sensitive data at unusual times or locations, downloading large amounts of data, or exhibiting unusual patterns of communication, it could be a sign of malicious intent or insider threat activity. Another approach to behavioral analysis for insider threat prevention is the use of data loss prevention (DLP) solutions, which focus on preventing unauthorized access to sensitive data and preventing data breaches caused by insiders. DLP solutions use a combination of content analysis, contextual analysis, and policy-based controls to monitor and control the movement of sensitive data within the organization. By analyzing data in real-time and applying policies to restrict access and prevent unauthorized sharing or exfiltration, DLP solutions can help organizations protect their sensitive information from insider threats. Endpoint detection and response (EDR) solutions also play a crucial role in behavioral analysis for insider threat prevention by monitoring endpoint devices for signs of malicious activity or unauthorized access. EDR solutions collect and analyze telemetry data from endpoint devices, such as process execution, file system activity, and network connections, to detect indicators of compromise (IOCs) and suspicious behavior. By correlating endpoint telemetry data with threat intelligence feeds and behavioral analytics, EDR solutions can identify potential insider threats and respond to security incidents in real-time. Privileged access management (PAM) solutions are another essential component of behavioral analysis for insider threat prevention, as insiders with privileged access pose a significant risk to organizations due to their elevated permissions and access to sensitive resources. PAM solutions help organizations manage and monitor privileged accounts and access rights, enforce least privilege principles, and detect and respond to unauthorized or suspicious activities performed by privileged users. By implementing PAM controls, organizations can reduce the risk of insider threats and prevent unauthorized access to critical systems and data. User activity monitoring (UAM) solutions are also important for behavioral analysis for insider threat prevention, as they capture and analyze user interactions with IT systems and applications to detect potential insider threats and policy violations. UAM solutions record user sessions, keystrokes, commands, and application activities, allowing organizations to monitor and audit user behavior in real-time. By analyzing user activity logs and correlating them with other security events and indicators, UAM solutions can detect suspicious behavior, such as unauthorized access attempts, data exfiltration, or policy violations, and alert security teams to potential insider threats. In summary, behavioral analysis is a critical component of insider threat prevention, as it enables organizations to proactively identify and mitigate the risks posed by insiders. By leveraging advanced techniques such as user behavior analytics, data loss prevention, endpoint detection and response, privileged access management, and user activity monitoring, organizations can detect and respond to insider threats in real-time, protect sensitive data and resources, and safeguard against the potentially devastating impact of insider attacks.

Chapter 8: Advanced Malware Analysis and Reverse Engineering

Dynamic malware analysis techniques involve the dynamic execution of suspicious files or programs in a controlled environment to observe their behavior and identify malicious activities. One commonly used dynamic analysis technique is sandboxing, which isolates the malware in a virtual environment to prevent it from affecting the host system. Sandboxing allows security researchers to execute the malware and monitor its behavior, such as file system modifications, network communication, and system calls, in a controlled manner. Sandboxing solutions often provide detailed reports and logs of the malware's activities, allowing analysts to analyze its behavior and identify indicators of compromise (IOCs). Another dynamic malware analysis technique is behavior-based analysis, which focuses on observing the actions and interactions of the malware with the operating system and other software components. Behavior-based analysis techniques monitor system events, such as process creation, file access, registry modifications, and network traffic, to identify suspicious behavior patterns indicative of malware activity. By analyzing these behavioral patterns, analysts can gain insights into the malware's functionality and intent and develop detection signatures or rules to identify similar threats in the future. Dynamic analysis techniques also include memory analysis, which involves analyzing the runtime memory of a process or application to identify malicious code or behavior. Memory analysis techniques allow analysts to examine the contents of the malware's memory space, including loaded modules, API calls, and data structures, to identify signs of malicious activity, such as code injection, process hollowing, or rootkit installation. Memory analysis tools, such as Volatility or Rekall, provide analysts with the ability to extract valuable information from the malware's memory space and uncover hidden artifacts or malware components. Another dynamic malware analysis technique is code emulation or instrumentation, which involves running the malware code in a simulated or emulated environment to observe its behavior and interactions with the underlying system. Code emulation techniques use specialized tools or frameworks, such as QEMU or Intel PIN, to execute the malware code in a controlled manner and monitor its execution flow, memory accesses, and system calls. By emulating the malware code, analysts can observe its behavior without risking infection of the host system and gain insights into its functionality and capabilities. Dynamic malware analysis techniques also include network traffic analysis, which involves monitoring and analyzing the network communication generated by the malware to identify command and control (C2) servers, data exfiltration channels, or other malicious activities. Network traffic analysis tools, such as Wireshark or tcpdump, capture and analyze network packets generated by the malware to identify patterns indicative of malicious behavior, such as unusual protocols, large data transfers, or suspicious domains. By analyzing the network traffic, analysts can identify the malware's communication patterns and infrastructure and develop countermeasures to block or mitigate its impact. In summary, dynamic malware analysis techniques play a crucial role in modern cybersecurity operations by enabling analysts to identify and analyze new and emerging threats in a timely and efficient manner. By leveraging techniques such as sandboxing, behavior-based analysis, memory analysis, code emulation, and network traffic analysis, analysts can gain insights into the behavior and capabilities of malware and develop effective detection and mitigation strategies to protect against cyber threats. Reverse engineering malicious code is a critical process in cybersecurity aimed at understanding the inner workings of malware to develop effective detection and mitigation strategies. One common technique used in reverse engineering is disassembly, which involves converting machine code into assembly language to analyze the instructions executed by the malware. Tools such as IDA Pro, Radare2, or Ghidra are commonly used for disassembly, allowing analysts to navigate through the code, identify functions, and understand the malware's behavior. Disassembly provides insights into the malware's logic flow, control structures, and function calls, helping analysts understand how the malware operates and how it interacts with the underlying system. Another important aspect of reverse engineering malicious code is static analysis, which involves analyzing the binary code of the malware without executing it. Static analysis techniques include examining file headers, extracting strings and resources, identifying imported and exported functions, and detecting code obfuscation or packing techniques. Static analysis tools such as PEiD, Exeinfo PE, or VirusTotal can assist analysts in extracting valuable information from the malware binary and identifying potential indicators of compromise (IOCs). Additionally, dynamic analysis techniques play a crucial role in reverse engineering malicious code by executing the malware in a controlled environment to observe its behavior. Dynamic analysis allows analysts to monitor the malware's interactions with the operating system, file system, registry, and network, providing insights into its functionality and intent. Tools such as Cuckoo Sandbox, FireEye's Mandiant Automated Defense (MAD), or Joe Sandbox automate the dynamic analysis process, allowing analysts to execute the malware safely and collect valuable telemetry data for analysis. In addition to disassembly, static analysis, and dynamic analysis, reverse engineers often use debugging techniques to gain insights into the malware's runtime behavior and execution flow. Debuggers such as OllyDbg, WinDbg, or x64dbg allow analysts to set breakpoints, inspect memory and register values, and step through the code to understand how the malware operates and to identify vulnerabilities or weaknesses. Reverse engineers also leverage code decompilation techniques to translate machine code into a higher-level programming language, making it easier to understand the malware's logic and functionality. Decompilers such as Hex-Rays IDA Pro with Hex-Rays Decompiler (IDA Hex-Rays), RetDec, or Ghidra's decompiler module can assist analysts in translating assembly code into C or C++ code, providing a higher-level abstraction of the malware's behavior. Moreover, reverse engineers often use data analysis techniques to extract and analyze data structures, encryption keys, or configuration settings embedded within the malware binary. Data analysis tools such as HxD, Binwalk, or CyberChef enable analysts to extract and manipulate data within the malware binary, allowing them to uncover hidden information and identify potential weaknesses or vulnerabilities. Another important aspect of reverse engineering malicious code is malware classification, which involves categorizing the malware based on its behavior, functionality, and intent. Malware classification enables analysts to understand the threat landscape better and to develop targeted detection and mitigation strategies for different types of malware. Overall, reverse engineering malicious code is a complex and multifaceted process that requires a combination of technical skills, tools, and techniques. By leveraging disassembly, static analysis, dynamic analysis, debugging, decompilation, data analysis, and malware classification techniques, reverse engineers can gain valuable insights into the inner workings of malware and develop effective countermeasures to protect against cyber threats.

Chapter 9: Security Metrics and Reporting

Key Performance Indicators (KPIs) for security operations play a vital role in assessing the effectiveness and efficiency of security measures implemented within an organization's infrastructure. One essential KPI is the mean time to detect (MTTD), which measures the average time taken to identify a security incident from its occurrence. Calculating MTTD involves recording the timestamps of when an incident is detected and when it actually occurred, then averaging these values across multiple incidents. This metric provides insights into how quickly security teams can identify and respond to potential threats, helping organizations improve their incident response capabilities. Another crucial KPI is the mean time to respond (MTTR), which measures the average time taken to mitigate and resolve a security incident once it has been detected. MTTR is calculated by recording the timestamps of when an incident is detected and when it is fully resolved, then averaging these values across multiple incidents. This metric enables organizations to assess the efficiency of their incident response processes and identify areas for improvement to minimize the impact of security breaches. Additionally, the number of false positives is an important KPI that measures the rate at which security alerts are generated incorrectly, leading to wasted time and resources investigating non-existent threats. By monitoring the number of false positives over time and identifying the root causes, organizations can fine-tune their security monitoring tools and processes to reduce false alarms and focus on genuine threats. Furthermore, the number of security incidents detected per unit of time is a critical KPI that helps organizations assess the overall threat landscape and the effectiveness of their security monitoring capabilities. By tracking the trend of security incidents over time, organizations can identify emerging threats and allocate resources more effectively to address potential vulnerabilities. Another essential KPI is the percentage of critical assets covered by security monitoring, which measures the proportion of an organization's most valuable and sensitive assets that are actively monitored for security threats. This metric helps organizations prioritize their security efforts and ensure that critical assets are adequately protected from potential cyber threats. Moreover, the mean time between failures (MTBF) is a valuable KPI that measures the average time elapsed between security incidents or system failures. By tracking MTBF over time, organizations can assess the reliability and resilience of their security infrastructure and identify areas for improvement to minimize downtime and disruptions. Additionally, the rate of security incidents per user or device is a useful KPI that helps organizations assess the security posture of individual users or devices within their network. By identifying users or devices with a high frequency of security incidents, organizations can implement targeted security measures such as additional training or security controls to reduce the risk of future incidents. Furthermore, the percentage of security alerts investigated is a critical KPI that measures the effectiveness of security teams in responding to alerts generated by security monitoring tools. By tracking the percentage of alerts investigated and comparing it to the total number of alerts generated, organizations can ensure that security teams are effectively triaging and prioritizing alerts to focus on the most significant threats. Additionally, the percentage of security incidents escalated to higher levels of management is an important KPI that measures the severity and impact of security incidents detected within an organization. By tracking the percentage of incidents escalated and analyzing the root causes, organizations can identify systemic issues and implement corrective actions to prevent future incidents. Moreover, the percentage of security incidents with documented root cause analysis (RCA) is a valuable KPI that measures the thoroughness of incident response processes and the effectiveness of corrective actions implemented. By ensuring that every security incident undergoes a detailed RCA, organizations can identify underlying vulnerabilities and weaknesses in their security posture and take proactive measures to address them. Additionally, the number of security incidents resolved without recurrence is an essential KPI that measures the effectiveness of corrective actions implemented in response to security incidents. By tracking the percentage of incidents resolved without recurrence and analyzing the root causes of recurring incidents, organizations can identify systemic issues and implement lasting solutions to prevent future incidents. Moreover, the percentage of security incidents with documented lessons learned is a valuable KPI that measures the effectiveness of knowledge sharing and continuous improvement within an organization's security operations. By documenting lessons learned from security incidents and disseminating them to relevant stakeholders, organizations can enhance their incident response capabilities and better prepare for future threats. Additionally, the percentage of security incidents with identified threat actors is an important KPI that helps organizations assess the sophistication and motivations of adversaries targeting their infrastructure. By tracking the percentage of incidents attributed to specific threat actors and analyzing their tactics, techniques, and procedures (TTPs), organizations can develop targeted countermeasures to defend against known threats. Moreover, the percentage of security incidents with identified indicators of compromise (IOCs) is a valuable KPI that measures the effectiveness of threat detection and incident response capabilities within an organization. By tracking the percentage of incidents with identified IOCs and analyzing their prevalence across multiple incidents, organizations can identify common attack patterns and develop proactive measures to detect and mitigate future threats. Additionally, the percentage of security incidents with identified vulnerabilities is an important KPI that helps organizations assess the overall security posture of their infrastructure.

Effective security reporting practices are essential for ensuring that stakeholders receive timely and accurate information about the organization's security posture and incidents. One key aspect of effective security reporting is the use of standardized formats and templates to ensure consistency and clarity in the information presented. For example, using a predefined template for incident reports helps ensure that all relevant details, such as the date and time of the incident, the affected systems or assets, and the actions taken in response, are consistently documented. This not only facilitates communication between security teams but also enables stakeholders to quickly understand the nature and severity of the incident. Additionally, security reports should be tailored to the specific audience receiving them, whether it's technical staff, executive management, or external stakeholders. For technical staff, reports may include detailed technical analysis and remediation steps, while executive management may require high-level summaries and recommendations for action. Similarly, external stakeholders such as regulatory agencies or customers may require reports that adhere to specific compliance standards or provide assurances about the organization's security posture. By customizing reports to meet the needs of different audiences, organizations can ensure that the information presented is relevant and actionable. Another important aspect of effective security reporting is the use of visualizations and graphical representations to convey complex information in a clear and understandable manner. For example, using charts, graphs, and dashboards to visualize trends in security incidents or vulnerabilities can help stakeholders quickly identify areas of concern and prioritize resources accordingly. Similarly, heat maps or risk matrices can provide a visual representation of the organization's risk landscape, highlighting areas of high risk that require immediate attention. By presenting information visually, organizations can enhance comprehension and decision-making and facilitate more effective communication about security issues. Furthermore, security reports should include actionable recommendations for addressing identified risks or vulnerabilities. These recommendations should be specific, measurable, achievable, relevant, and time-bound (SMART), making it clear what steps need to be taken and by when. For example, if a vulnerability is identified during a security assessment, the report should include recommendations for patching or mitigating the vulnerability, along with a timeline for implementation. Similarly, if an incident reveals gaps in security controls or processes, the report should include recommendations for remediation and improvement. By providing actionable recommendations, security reports empower stakeholders to take proactive steps to enhance the organization's security posture and mitigate risks. Additionally, security reports should be issued regularly and in a timely manner to ensure that stakeholders are kept informed of the latest developments and emerging threats. Depending on the organization's risk profile and regulatory requirements, reports may be issued daily, weekly, monthly, or quarterly. Regardless of the frequency, it's essential to establish a consistent reporting cadence and adhere to it to maintain transparency and accountability. Furthermore, security reports should be reviewed and validated by appropriate stakeholders before being distributed. This ensures that the information presented is accurate, complete, and relevant, and that any recommendations or actions proposed are feasible and appropriate. By involving key stakeholders in the review process, organizations can ensure that security reports are credible and trusted sources of information. Additionally, security reports should include a mechanism for tracking and monitoring the implementation of recommendations and actions. This allows stakeholders to follow up on progress and ensure that identified risks or vulnerabilities are being addressed in a timely manner. For example, reports may include a status dashboard or progress tracker that indicates the current status of each recommendation, along with any outstanding issues or barriers to implementation. By providing visibility into the status of remediation efforts, organizations can hold stakeholders accountable and ensure that security improvements are effectively implemented. Moreover, security reports should be archived and retained for future reference and audit purposes. Depending on regulatory requirements and organizational policies, reports may need to be retained for a certain period of time, typically ranging from several months to several years. By maintaining a comprehensive archive of security reports, organizations can demonstrate compliance with regulatory requirements, track historical trends in security incidents and vulnerabilities, and facilitate post-incident analysis and learning. In summary, effective security reporting practices are essential for ensuring that stakeholders receive timely, accurate, and actionable information about the organization's security posture and incidents. By using standardized formats, tailoring reports to the specific needs of different audiences, visualizing complex information, providing actionable recommendations, issuing reports regularly and in a timely manner, involving key stakeholders in the review process, tracking implementation progress, and retaining reports for future reference, organizations can enhance transparency, accountability, and effectiveness in managing security risks.

Chapter 10: Emerging Trends in Security Operations

Next-Generation Security Operations Centers (SOCs) represent a significant evolution in the way organizations detect, respond to, and mitigate cybersecurity threats. These advanced SOCs leverage cutting-edge technologies, processes, and methodologies to enhance threat detection capabilities, improve incident response times, and strengthen overall cybersecurity posture. One key aspect of next-generation SOCs is their focus on proactive threat hunting, which involves actively searching for signs of compromise and anomalous behavior within an organization's network and systems. This proactive approach allows security teams to identify and address potential threats before they escalate into full-blown security incidents. To deploy threat hunting techniques effectively, security teams can utilize specialized tools and platforms that enable them to collect and analyze large volumes of security data from various sources, such as network traffic logs, endpoint telemetry, and threat intelligence feeds. For example, the command grep can be used to search for specific patterns or indicators of compromise within log files, while the Suricata intrusion detection system can be deployed to monitor network traffic for suspicious activity. In addition to threat hunting, next-generation SOCs also prioritize automation and orchestration to streamline security operations and improve efficiency. By automating routine tasks such as incident triage, malware analysis, and vulnerability scanning, security teams can free up valuable time and resources to focus on more strategic initiatives. This automation can be achieved using scripting languages such as Python or by deploying specialized security orchestration, automation, and response (SOAR) platforms that integrate with existing security tools and systems. For example, the Python scripting language can be used to develop custom automation scripts that automate repetitive tasks, while the Splunk Phantom platform can be used to orchestrate incident response workflows and automate response actions. Moreover, next-generation SOCs place a strong emphasis on data-driven decision-making and threat intelligence integration. By aggregating, correlating, and analyzing security data from various sources, including internal logs, external feeds, and open-source intelligence, security teams can gain valuable insights into emerging threats and attack trends. These insights enable organizations to make informed decisions about their security posture and prioritize security investments accordingly. To integrate threat intelligence effectively into security operations, organizations can leverage threat intelligence platforms that provide centralized management, enrichment, and sharing of threat intelligence feeds. For example, the MISP platform can be used to aggregate and share threat intelligence feeds with internal security teams and external partners, while the STIX/TAXII standards can be used to exchange threat intelligence information between different security tools and platforms.

Furthermore, next-generation SOCs emphasize collaboration and information sharing both within the organization and across industry sectors. By fostering a culture of collaboration and knowledge sharing, security teams can leverage the collective expertise and experience of the broader security community to identify and mitigate threats more effectively. This collaboration can take various forms, including participating in information sharing and analysis centers (ISACs), attending industry conferences and workshops, and collaborating with peer organizations on joint threat hunting initiatives. Additionally, next-generation SOCs prioritize continuous improvement and innovation to stay ahead of evolving threats and challenges. By regularly assessing and updating their tools, processes, and procedures, security teams can adapt to changing threat landscapes and emerging attack techniques. This continuous improvement mindset encourages experimentation and innovation, enabling organizations to develop new and innovative approaches to threat detection, response, and mitigation. Overall, next-generation SOCs represent a fundamental shift in how organizations approach cybersecurity operations, leveraging advanced technologies, processes, and methodologies to enhance threat detection, response, and mitigation capabilities. By adopting a proactive approach to threat hunting, prioritizing automation and orchestration, integrating threat intelligence, fostering collaboration and information sharing, and embracing a culture of continuous improvement and innovation, organizations can build resilient and adaptive security operations that are well-equipped to defend against today's sophisticated cyber threats. Threat intelligence sharing platforms play a crucial role in enhancing cybersecurity by facilitating the exchange of threat intelligence information among organizations, security vendors, government agencies, and other stakeholders. These platforms serve as central repositories where organizations can contribute, access, and collaborate on threat intelligence data, including indicators of compromise (IOCs), malware signatures, attack patterns, and other relevant information. One of the key benefits of threat intelligence sharing platforms is their ability to provide organizations with access to a diverse range of threat intelligence feeds and sources, allowing them to gain insights into emerging threats and vulnerabilities that they may not have been aware of otherwise. By aggregating and correlating threat intelligence data from multiple sources, these platforms enable organizations to build a more comprehensive understanding of the current threat landscape and identify potential security risks proactively. Moreover, threat intelligence sharing platforms promote collaboration and information sharing among organizations, helping to foster a collective defense approach to cybersecurity. Through these platforms, organizations can share insights, best practices, and actionable intelligence with their peers, enabling them to collectively defend against common threats and adversaries. This collaborative approach is particularly valuable for industries or sectors that face similar cybersecurity challenges, such as financial services, healthcare, or critical infrastructure. Additionally, threat intelligence sharing platforms can help organizations improve their incident response capabilities by providing real-time threat intelligence feeds and alerts. By integrating threat intelligence directly into their security operations workflows, organizations can automate the detection, triage, and response to security incidents more effectively. For example, threat intelligence sharing platforms often support integration with security orchestration, automation, and response (SOAR) tools, allowing organizations to automatically enrich security alerts with threat intelligence data and orchestrate response actions based on predefined playbooks. Furthermore, threat intelligence sharing platforms play a crucial role in supporting regulatory compliance and industry standards. Many regulations and standards, such as the General Data Protection Regulation (GDPR), the Payment Card Industry Data Security Standard (PCI DSS), and the Health Insurance Portability and Accountability Act (HIPAA), require organizations to implement measures for threat detection, incident response, and information sharing. By leveraging threat intelligence sharing platforms, organizations can demonstrate compliance with these requirements by demonstrating their ability to access and share relevant threat intelligence data with authorized parties. Deploying a threat intelligence sharing platform typically involves several steps, starting with the selection of a suitable platform that meets the organization's requirements in terms of features, functionality, and scalability. Once a platform has been selected, organizations need to onboard their security teams and other relevant stakeholders, providing them with access to the platform and training them on how to use it effectively. Additionally, organizations need to establish policies and procedures for contributing and accessing threat intelligence data, ensuring that sensitive information is handled securely and in compliance with relevant regulations and industry standards. This may involve implementing access controls, encryption, and other security measures to protect the confidentiality, integrity, and availability of threat intelligence data. Furthermore, organizations should establish processes for sharing threat intelligence with trusted partners and third-party vendors, establishing clear guidelines for how information should be shared, what types of information can be shared, and under what circumstances sharing is permitted. Finally, organizations should regularly review and update their threat intelligence sharing practices to ensure that they remain effective and relevant in the face of evolving threats and challenges. By following these best practices and deploying a robust threat intelligence sharing platform, organizations can enhance their cybersecurity posture and better defend against the growing threat of cyber attacks.

Conclusion

In summary, the "Security+ Exam Pass: (SY0-701) Security Architecture, Threat Identification, Risk Management, Operations" book bundle offers a comprehensive and cohesive approach to preparing for the SY0-701 exam. Through four distinct volumes, readers are guided through the essential concepts, strategies, and techniques necessary to excel in the field of cybersecurity.

In "Foundations of Security Architecture: A Beginner's Guide to SY0-701," readers are introduced to the fundamental principles of security architecture, providing them with a solid understanding of the building blocks of secure systems and networks. This book serves as a cornerstone for individuals looking to establish a strong foundation in cybersecurity.

"Mastering Threat Identification: Strategies and Techniques for SY0-701" delves into the intricacies of threat identification, equipping readers with the knowledge and skills needed to identify and mitigate various types of cybersecurity threats. From malware analysis to threat hunting methodologies, this volume empowers readers to stay ahead of evolving cyber threats.

"Risk Management Essentials: Navigating Security Challenges in SY0-701" explores the critical role of risk management in cybersecurity, offering practical guidance on assessing, prioritizing, and mitigating security risks. By understanding the principles of risk management, readers are better equipped to make informed decisions and allocate resources effectively to protect their organizations.

Finally, "Advanced Security Operations: Implementing SY0-701 Best Practices and Beyond" takes readers beyond the basics, delving into advanced security operations and best practices. From incident response planning to security automation, this volume provides readers with the tools and techniques needed to streamline security operations and respond effectively to security incidents.

Collectively, these four volumes offer a comprehensive and holistic approach to preparing for the SY0-701 exam and mastering the essential concepts and practices of cybersecurity. Whether you're a beginner looking to establish a solid foundation or an experienced professional seeking to enhance your skills, the "Security+ Exam Pass: (SY0-701) Security Architecture, Threat Identification, Risk Management, Operations" book bundle is an invaluable resource for anyone looking to succeed in the dynamic and ever-evolving field of cybersecurity.